SERIES TEACHING FILM AND MEDIA STUDIES

Teaching TV Drama

Jeremy Points

Series Editor: Vivienne Clark
Commissioning Editor: Wendy Earle

British Library Cataloguing-in-Publication Data
A catalogue record for this guide is available from the British Library

ISBN 1 84457 132 7

First published in 2007 by the British Film Institute
21 Stephen Street, London W1T 1LN

Student worksheets to support this guide are supplied at: www.bfi.org.uk/tfms
User name: **tvdrama@bfi.org.uk** Password: **te0310dr**

Design: Amanda Hawkes
Cover photograph: David Threlfall in *Shameless*, courtesy of *bfi* Stills
Printed in Great Britain by: Cromwell Press Ltd

www.bfi.org.uk
There's more to discover about film and television through the BFI.
Our world-renowned archive, cinemas, festivals, films, publications
and learning resources are here to inspire you.

Contents

Introduction to the series

Since the introduction of the revised post-16 qualifications (AS and A2 Level) in the UK in September 2000, the number of students taking A Level Film and Media Studies has increased significantly. For example, the latest entry statistics show the following trend:

Subject & Level	June 2001	June 2002	June 2005
A Level Film Studies+	2,017	–	–
AS Level Film Studies	3,852	–	9,188
A2 Level Film Studies	–	2,175	4,913
A Level Media Studies*+	16,293	–	–
AS Level Media Studies*	22,872	–	32,346
A2 Level Media Studies*	–	18,150	23,427

* Three combined awarding bodies' results
† Legacy syllabus – last entry June 2001
(Source: BFI Education website – AS/A2 statistics refer to cashed-in entries only)

Furthermore, changes to the 14–19 curriculum currently in development for 2008 will doubtless see further increases in the take-up of courses (and indeed new courses) in this popular subject area. In response to the continuing expansion of this subject area (unabated despite criticisms from ill-informed pundits), a professional association of media educators in the UK (MEA – www.mediaedassociation.org.uk) has been formed to support teachers at all levels and in all learning contexts, as well as to provide much-needed accurate public relations information and guidance about the many courses on offer and how to differentiate between them.

Inevitably these increases in student numbers have led to a pressing demand for more teachers and both new and experienced teachers (from other disciplines) alike may be faced with teaching these subjects for the first time, without necessarily a degree-level background to help them with subject content and conceptual understanding. In addition, frequently changing specifications see the arrival of new set topics and areas of study, so there is a continued need for up-to-date resources to help teacher preparation. Media study is best when it responds to current media output and issues and it is our aim to provide reference to recent media texts and products as well as to older ones.

I developed the concept and format of this series with the above factors, and busy and enthusiastic teachers (and creative and energetic students), in mind. Each title provides an accessible reference resource, with essential topic content, as well as clear guidance on good classroom practice to improve the quality of teaching and students' learning. We are confident that, as well as supporting the teacher new to these subjects, the series provides the experienced specialist with new critical perspectives and teaching approaches as well as useful content.

The two sample schemes of work included in Section 1 are intended as practical models to help get teachers started. They are not prescriptive, as any effective scheme of work has to be developed with the specific requirements of an assessment context, and ability of the teaching group, in mind. Likewise, the worksheets provided in the online materials offer examples of good practice, which can be adapted to your specific needs and contexts. In some cases, the online resources include interviews and illustrative material, as webnotes. See www.bfi.org.uk/tfms.

The series is clear evidence of the range, depth and breadth of teacher expertise and specialist knowledge required at A Level in these subjects. Also, it is an affirmation of why this subject area is such an important, rich and compelling one for increasing numbers of 16- to 19-year-old students. Many of the more theoretical titles in the series include reference to practical exercises involving media production skills. It is important that it is understood here that the current A Levels in Media and Film Studies are not designed as vocational, or prevocational, qualifications. In these contexts, the place of practical media production is to offer students active, creative and engaging ways in which to explore theory and reflect on their own practice.

It has been very gratifying to see that several titles in this series have found an international audience, in the USA, Canada and Australia, among others, and we hope that future titles continue to be of interest in international moving image education. Every author in the series is an experienced teacher of Film and/or Media Studies at this level and many have examining/moderating experience. It has been a pleasure to work so closely with such a diverse range of committed professionals and I should like to thank them for their individual contributions to this expanding series.

Vivienne Clark
Series Editor
November 2006

● Key features

- Assessment contexts for the major UK post-16 Film and Media Studies specifications
- Suggested schemes of work
- Historical contexts (where appropriate)
- Key facts, statistics and terms
- Detailed reference to the key concepts of Film and Media Studies
- Detailed case studies
- Glossaries
- Bibliographies
- Student worksheets, activities and resources (available online) – ready to print and photocopy for the classroom.

● Other titles in the series:

- *Teaching Scriptwriting, Screenplays and Storyboards for Film and TV Production* (Mark Readman);
- *Teaching TV Sitcom* (James Baker);
- *Teaching Digital Video Production* (Pete Fraser and Barney Oram);
- *Teaching TV News* (Eileen Lewis);
- *Teaching Women and Film* (Sarah Gilligan);
- *Teaching World Cinema* (Kate Gamm);
- *Teaching TV Soaps* (Lou Alexander and Alison Cousens);
- *Teaching Contemporary British Broadcasting* (Rachel Viney);
- *Teaching Contemporary British Cinema* (Sarah Casey Benyahia);
- *Teaching Music Video* (Pete Fraser);
- *Teaching Auteur Study* (David Wharton and Jeremy Grant);
- *Teaching Analysis of Film Language* (David Wharton and Jeremy Grant);
- *Teaching Men and Film* (Matthew Hall);
- *Teaching Film Censorship and Controversy* (Mark Readman);
- *Teaching Stars and Performance* (Jill Poppy);
- *Teaching Video Games* (James Newman and Barney Oram);
- *Teaching Black Cinema* (Peter Jones).

● Forthcoming titles include:

- *Teaching Short Films*; *Teaching Film and TV Documentary*.

There is also an associated shorter series aimed at GCSE Media Studies, GCSE English and other relevant media-related courses for 14–16-year-olds.

SERIES EDITOR: Vivienne Clark is a teacher of Film and Media Studies at Langley Park School for Boys, Beckenham, Kent, and an Advanced Skills Teacher. She is currently an Associate Tutor of BFI Education and formerly a

Principal Examiner for A Level Media Studies for one of the English awarding bodies. She is also a freelance teacher trainer, media education consultant and writer/editor, with several published textbooks and resources, including *GCSE Media Studies* (Longman 2002), *Key Concepts and Skills for Media Studies* (Hodder Arnold, 2002) and *The Complete A–Z Film and Media Studies Handbook* (Hodder and Stoughton, 2007). She is also a course tutor for the BFI/Institute of Education MA module, An Introduction to Media Education Practice.

AUTHOR: Jeremy Points is currently the Subject Officer for Media and Film at the WJEC. He was previously Head of Media, Film and Communication Studies at a sixth-form college in Brighton and an examiner for A Level Media and A Level Communication Studies. The author of a study guide on *American Beauty* (Auteur, 2004), he has provided INSETs in a variety of contexts, including the annual conferences for Media and Film Studies organised by the BFI and Media Education Wales.

Introduction

Assessment contexts

Awarding body & level	Subject	Unit code	Module/Topic
✓ AQA AS Level	Media Studies	Med 1	Reading the Media
✓ AQA AS Level	Media Studies	Med 2	Textual Topics in Contemporary Media: Film and Broadcast Fiction
✓ AQA A2 Level	Media Studies	Med 4	Texts and Contexts in the Media
✓ AQA A2 Level	Media Studies	Med 5	Independent Study
✓ AQA A2 Level	Media Studies	Med 6	Comparative Critical Analysis
✓ EdExcel AVCE	Media: Communication and Production	Unit 1	Media Analysis
✓ EdExcel AVCE	Media: Communication and Production	Unit 6	Media Industries
✓ OCR A2 Level	Media Studies	2734	Critical Research Study (TV drama)
✓ OCR A2 Level	Media Studies	2735	Media Issues and Debates: British Broadcasting in the 1990s
✓ WJEC AS Level	Media Studies	ME1	Modern Media Forms
✓ WJEC AS Level	Media Studies	ME2	Media Representations and Reception
✓ WJEC A2 Level	Media Studies	ME4	Investigating Media Texts
✓ WJEC A2 Level	Media Studies	ME5	Changing Media Industries
✓ WJEC A2 Level	Media Studies	ME6	Text and Context
✓ SQA Higher	Media Studies	DF 14	12 Media Analysis: Fiction (Higher)
✓ SQA Advanced Higher	Media Studies	DV 31	13 Media Analysis
✓ SQA Advanced Higher	Media Studies	DV 32	13 Media Investigation

This guide is also relevant to the various vocational and applied specifications, as well as to international and lifelong learning courses.

Other guides in this series offer excellent complementary information to this guide:
- *Teaching Contemporary British Broadcasting* (Rachel Viney)
- *Teaching TV Sitcom* (James Baker)
- *Teaching TV Soaps* (Lou Alexander and Alison Cousens)
- *Teaching Scriptwriting, Screenplays and Storyboards for Film and TV Production* (Mark Readman)

Other BFI resources which support this topic include:
- BFI's new series of TV Classics, featuring TV drama series such as *Dr Who* and *The Office.*
- *Tele-Visions: An Introduction to Studying Television*, Glen Creeber
- *The Television Genre Book*, edited by Glen Creeber

● Specification links

The study of TV drama outlined in this guide is relevant to the following specification areas:

AQA AS Level Media Studies
- MED1 Reading the Media: This guide provides analysis and application of all the key concepts students are required to study for this module. The key media concepts specified are: representations, media language (including genre and narrative), values and ideology, institutions and audiences.
- MED2 Textual Topics in Contemporary Media: Film and Broadcast Fiction is one of the set topics for this module: the study of two broadcast fiction texts is required. The case studies can be used as the basis for studying two contemporary TV dramas while the approach outlined in Section 2 is designed to provide a general approach to any TV drama through the key media concepts.

AQA A2 Level Media Studies
- MED 4 Texts and Contexts in the Media: This guide provides the basis for studying three of the four set topics in this module (representations, genre and media audiences).
- MED5 Independent Study: The independent study is focused on contemporary media texts and topics arising from them. This guide should provide a framework for students' independent research into contemporary media, and any of the case studies could provide a starting point.
- MED6 Comparative Critical Analysis: This module requires the comparative study of two media texts. The study is based on applying the relevant key media concepts to the two texts – media concepts which underlie this guide.

EdExcel AVCE in Media: Communication and Production

- Unit 1 Media Analysis: Analysing media texts, representation, genre and narrative. This guide provides examples of analysing media texts in the way specified in this unit.
- Unit 6 Media Industries: Ownership and regulatory controls, production and distribution affected by ownership and technological changes, globalisation. There are numerous references in Section 2, in particular, to the relationship between producing organisations, broadcasters as distributors and TV drama, as well as examples of the impact of technological developments on TV drama.

OCR A2 Level Media Studies

- Unit 2734 Critical Research Study (TV drama): The general approach taken in Section 2 should provide students with a framework for any study they might choose. The case studies could provide starting points for their own research.
- Unit 2735 Media Issues and Debates (British Broadcasting in the 1990s): The guide provides background and relevant case studies on the broadcasting industry in Britain.

WJEC AS Level Media Studies

- ME1 Modern Media Forms: Requires students to develop analytical skills through studying a range of media forms. The approach to TV drama in this guide can be used to explore the television form.
- ME2 Media Representations and Reception: A general approach to representation relevant to ME2 is included in Section 2, while representation issues are included in the majority of the case studies in Section 3.

WJEC A2 Level Media Studies

- ME4 Investigating Media Texts: Requires research into media texts in relation to one of the key media concepts (genre, narrative and representation). Section 2 approaches TV drama through those key concepts, and Section 3 could provide starting points for an investigation based on TV drama.
- ME5 Changing Media Industries: Television is one of the industries which can be studied. Students are required to study television programmes as a way of exploring industry and audience issues. This guide takes that approach to TV drama.
- ME6 Text and Context: The set topic for 2006–8 is the crime genre. There are several references to crime in Section 2 and Case Study 1 is based on crime. All crime dramas are explored through the key contexts of institutions and audiences, which students are required to study for this unit.

SQA Higher/Advanced Higher Media Studies

- DF14 12 Media Analysis: (Fiction): The concepts at the root of this guide should enable students to apply them to the analysis of all broadcast fiction as the specification requires.
- DV31 13 Media Analysis: This guide approaches TV drama using the same basic concepts of contexts, texts and audiences and could therefore be adapted to the requirements of the unit.
- DV32 13 Media Investigation: Several of the issues specified for investigation are dealt with in this guide and could therefore be adapted to it.

What is TV drama? Basic definitions

Drama is a Greek word and according to a Greek philosopher, Aristotle, it meant action. By action, he meant something acted out to communicate a message. What he was describing therefore was action in the form of a story. We could therefore describe TV drama as fictionalised action in narrative form produced for television.

More than most other television genres, TV drama is a broad category, covering several different kinds of drama (everything from soap opera to classic literary adaptations) as well as several different narrative forms (ranging from single dramas, two-parters and mini-series to the various kinds of long-form drama such as serials, series and continuing dramas). This proliferation of drama into different types – subgenres – has its roots in the 1950s when the BBC and later ITV attempted to attract different kinds of audiences. It was during this period that the first children's serials, classic dramas, crime dramas, medical series and adventure series appeared. Despite this variety of subgenres, broadcasting organisations still label their diverse kinds of drama 'TV drama' and promote them as such (look at the BBC's website, its former ident 'The One for Drama' or ITV's sponsored 'drama strands').

What links all these forms of TV drama is the way they use characters to tell a story. The continuing popularity of the genre and its importance to broadcasters seems to be rooted in people's fascination with, and emotional involvement in, characters and stories. This interest is of course culturally conditioned. The film and media industries' continual investment in drama ensures that people's appetite for it is constantly renewed.

In studying TV drama, students need to recognise the relationship between the genre as a whole, highly significant to broadcasters, and the way it has developed on television, which has given rise to different subgenres and correspondingly different audiences.

● Controversial status?

One of the interesting aspects of this topic – and one of the reasons for its breadth – is that the genre has always given rise to controversy both inside and outside broadcasting organisations. That controversy has been rooted in arguments about high and low culture – the high prestige of the single-authored drama (which the BBC is due to reintroduce as a strand in 2007) and literary adaptations, for example, versus the supposedly lower prestige of soap operas or the popular, sometimes sensationally melodramatic, drama series (often viewed as an economic compromise). Although elements of that debate continue to be reflected in the way broadcasters themselves equate 'quality' with certain kinds of drama for their own purposes (commercial, audience reach, convincing the government of public service remit), this guide takes a contemporary, pluralist approach, recognising that no one form of drama has an inherently higher value than any other and that different audiences find different values in the dramas they watch.

Why study TV drama?

● Products, institutions and audiences

As a genre, TV drama is vital to television, attracting large audiences and thus providing media students with an accessible way of approaching the key concepts underlying all study of the media.

During the takeover of Company TV in 2004, Steve Morrison, Chief Executive of All3Media, described drama as the 'biggest genre in British television'. It is television's 'film' and, like film, TV drama reaches large, frequently global audiences. In a digitally converging environment, where new platforms are providing new forms such as 'mobisodes' and interactive drama, and new means of distribution such as downloadable drama, the impact of the genre is set to continue. It is thus important to ask questions about TV drama programmes to find out how audiences relate to them and what kind of influence they may have.

Within Media Studies, these questions have characteristically been explored through studying the relationship between media products, their institutional contexts and their audiences. This relationship lies at the root of all specifications for AS/A Level, Scottish Highers and applied qualifications.

Studying TV drama will thus allow students to see clearly:

- how institutions – producing organisations and broadcasters – and audiences shape media products like TV drama;
- the different ways audiences respond to the media;
- how far the media influences the way people think and feel.

How to use this guide

● Approach and the use of theories

It is important to encourage students to understand the significance of theories, but also to raise questions about them rather than basing analysis on theories alone.

Generally speaking, the guide attempts to integrate theoretical perspectives into teaching and examples, referring explicitly to some of the familiar theoretical perspectives but also focusing on the ideas underlying them rather than applying them in detail. It is important to encourage students to understand the significance of theories and to raise questions about them rather than placing the sole emphasis on theories. Some theoretical approaches, which necessarily involve simplification at AS and A Level, are more valuable for students than others and this will be reflected in the approach adopted here. However, the guide also points teachers to sources of support if they wish to explore particular theories in more detail.

● Organisation of the guide

Section 2, 'Background', explores a range of TV dramas through the key media concepts of genre, narrative, realism, representation, institutions and audiences, and is designed to be applicable to any case study material teachers may wish to select. Section 3, 'Case studies', highlights different key concepts in relation to each of the following dramas, although representation, arguably the concept at the centre of Media Studies informs them all:

- Crime drama as subgenre (*Life on Mars* and *CSI: NY*): how broadcasters approach a popular subgenre; how genre affects representation issues;
- Literary adaptation (*Bleak House*): how broadcasters make a niche genre more widely accessible;
- Drama from the popular mainstream (*Spooks*): genre, narrative and representation issues;
- 'Family' sci-fi drama (*Doctor Who*): audience responses to representation issues; fans;
- Alternative, challenging drama (*Shameless* and *Six Feet Under*): broadcasters and representation.

● Reasons for this focus

The guide concentrates on recent TV dramas, most of which are still being screened on British terrestrial television, but also includes reference to a number of significant dramas from the past. TV drama is available in the Background section and on the website.

This guide does not include case study material on children's or teen drama (apart from the 'family' drama *Doctor Who*), sensational popular melodramas like *Footballers' Wives* and *Desperate Housewives* or long-form dramas like *24*, *Lost* or *Invasion*, predicated on narrative enigmas.

● Websites

Worksheets have been developed to support the suggestions in this guide. You can access these through the website: www.bfi.org.uk/tfms. Click on the title of this guide and then enter the User name: **tvdrama@bfi.org.uk** Password: **te0310dr**

Additional materials are available on the website linked to this volume, but there is also an excellent range of key extracts from TV dramas past and present as well as short overviews of topics on the BFI's *Screenonline* www.bfi.screenonline. These extracts can be: played by individual students, as part of their research; played through an interactive whiteboard; or downloaded for susequent classroom use.

Schemes of work

The schemes of work are set out in stages and represent six weeks of approximately 4hrs 30mins teaching time per week with one teacher. Clearly this is approximately 12 weeks of 2hrs 15mins if you are sharing the teaching for a group.

● Scheme of work 1: Exploring the crime genre

The first scheme of work:

- Focuses on one subgenre (crime – see Section 3) and suggests three main case studies;
- Explores genre, narrative and representation, integrating this with audience response;
- Raises institutional issues based on the case studies.

Aims:
On completing this unit students should be able to
- Exhibit a good understanding of contemporary crime drama;
- Understand and apply the fundamental concepts of media, genre, narrative and representation to a range of crime dramas;
- Understand the way industry and audiences shape media products like crime dramas and be able to speculate on the relationship between crime dramas and audiences.

Outcomes:

- An analysis of a range of crime dramas in relation to the key concepts of genre, narrative and representation;
- An understanding of how dominant ideologies are either reinforced or challenged;
- A recognition of the different ways different audiences respond to crime dramas;
- An appreciation of how crime dramas may shape audiences' points of view.

Week 1

Establish a basic understanding of TV drama and its conventions
Establish an understanding of the way genres are open to change and break down into subgenres
Raise questions about the reasons for exploring the genre
Introduce crime drama and establish its specific conventions
Worksheets 1, 2 and 3

Week 2

Genre as repetition and variation: broadcasters' approach to the genre
Development of the genre through the schematic history of significant crime dramas from the past
Case study 1: a conventional crime drama – its narrative and representation issues
Audience positioning
(Suggestions: *Dalziel and Pascoe*, *Frost*, *Rebus*, *CSI*, *The Closer*, *Midsomer Murders*)
Worksheets 3, 4, 5, 6, 16 and 17

Week 3

Case study 2: a second, textually more complex conventional drama with hybrid features (focus more on approach to realism, representation and ideology)
Raise audience issues: notably, the way different audiences respond differently to representations and their underlying ideologies
(Suggestions: *Messiah 4*, *Blackpool*, *Prime Suspect* 6 or 7, *The Shield*)
Worksheets 9, 10, 11, 12 and 13

Week 4

Institutional issues drawn from Case studies 1 and 2, with additional extracts
Factors affecting production
Relationship between producers and broadcasters
Exploring how broadcasters use crime drama (channel identity, scheduling, attracting and maintaining audiences, marketing, promotion and sponsorship,

acquisitions and overseas sales, sell-through, role of websites and potential audience interaction)

Role of different formats and their implications for audiences (on-demand viewing, DVD sales, downloading, mobisodes)

Worksheets 14 and 15

Week 5

Case study 3: an alternative and more challenging crime drama

Focus on representation, ideology and audience issues as a way of isolating alternative features

(Suggestions: *The Sopranos*, *Conviction*)

Worksheets 8, 21 and 27

Week 6

Audience issues arising from all three case studies

Looking at the way industry and audience issues shape TV dramas

Thinking about the relationship between TV dramas and audiences: constructing, determining, providing frameworks for, shaping points of view and ideologies?

Worksheets 8, 13 and 27

- ## Scheme of work 2: TV drama from the popular mainstream to the alternative and challenging

The second scheme of work:

- Explores one example of a popular mainstream drama from the point of view of genre, narrative and representation, institution and audience (eg, *Spooks* – see Case study 3);
- Develops each main concept with a cluster of shorter case studies, as in this guide, to provide an overview of the breadth of the TV drama genre;
- Explores one example of an alternative, more challenging drama (eg, *Shameless* or *Six Feet Under* – see Case study 5).

Aims: On completing this unit, students should be able to:

- Exhibit a good understanding of contemporary TV drama;
- Understand and apply the fundamental concepts of media, genre, narrative and representation to a range of TV dramas;
- Understand the way industry and audiences shape media products like TV dramas and be able to speculate on the relationship between TV dramas and audiences.

Outcomes:

- Analysis of a range of TV dramas in relation to the key concepts of genre, narrative and representation;

- An understanding of how dominant ideologies are either reinforced or challenged;
- A recognition of the different ways different audiences respond to TV dramas;
- An appreciation of how TV dramas may shape audiences' points of view.

Week 1

Establish a basic understanding of TV drama and its conventions
Establish an understanding of the way genres are open to change and break down into subgenres
Raise questions about the reasons for exploring the genre
Introduce a drama from the popular mainstream and establish the conventions of TV drama in more detail/its appropriate subgenre
Worksheets 1, 2 and 3

Week 2

Genre as repetition and variation: broadcasters' approach to the genre
Development of the genre through the schematic history of significant crime dramas from the past
Case study 1: a drama from the popular mainstream – its narrative and representational issues
Audience positioning
(Suggestions: *Spooks*, *Hustle*, *ER*, *Doctor Who*, *Footballers' Wives*)
Worksheets 3, 4, 5, 6, 20, 21, 22, 23 and 24

Week 3

Case study 2: a second, textually more complex conventional drama with hybrid features (focus more on approach to realism, representation and ideology)
Raise audience issues: notably, the way different audiences respond differently to representations and their underlying ideologies
(Suggestions: *Desperate Housewives*, *Blackpool*, *State of Play*, *The Street*)
Worksheets 9, 10, 11, 12 and13

Week 4

Institutional issues drawn from Case studies 1 and 2, with additional extracts
Factors affecting production
Relationship between producers and broadcasters
Exploring how broadcasters use crime drama (channel identity, scheduling, attracting and maintaining audiences, marketing, promotion and sponsorship, acquisitions and overseas sales, sell-through, role of websites and potential audience interaction)
Role of different formats and their implications for audiences (on-demand viewing, DVD sales, downloading, mobisodes)
Worksheets 14 and 15

Week 5

Case study 3: an alternative and more challenging drama

Focus on representation, ideology and audience issues as a way of isolating alternative features

(Suggestions: *The Sopranos*, *Shameless*, *Six Feet Under*, *Funland*)

Worksheets 8, 21 and 27

Week 6

Audience issues arising from all three case studies

Looking at the way industry and audience issues shape TV dramas

Thinking about the relationship between TV dramas and audiences: constructing, determining, providing frameworks for, shaping points of view and ideologies.

Worksheets 8, 13 and 27

Background

Timeline: TV Drama in Britain

This timeline is available as a downloadable pdf (see www.bfi.org.uk/tfms
Username: **tvdrama@bfi.org.uk** Password: **te0310dr**).

1922	British Broadcasting Company Ltd founded.
1923	First full-length play broadcast on radio.
1927	British Broadcasting Corporation founded – public service (radio) broadcasting established.
1930	First experiment in televising a play: *The Man with a Flower in His Mouth*, by the surrealist Italian playwright Luigi Pirandello.
1936	First television broadcast (television broadcasting was suspended between 1940 and 1946 because of World War II).
1940s	TV drama is televised theatre, with very simple studio camerawork, and comprises 'one-off' plays.
1946 – 47	TV drama becomes a significant element of programming. JB Priestley's *Rose and Crown* (BBC), set in a pub, was innovative as it portrayed a working-class world on television almost for the first time.
1947–1950	Two different productions of Patrick Hamilton's *Rope* (BBC), a good example of the more usual portrayal of a middle-class world on television. (Relocated from its original Oxford setting to Yale University and the US, it was filmed by Alfred Hitchcock in 1948.)
1950s	TV drama diversifies. The main subgenres familiar to today's audiences are established – crime, hospital, children's drama, the classic serial, sci-fi and soaps. Drama series and serials are introduced alongside plays, still an important part of TV drama output.
1954–57	First police series: *Fabian of Scotland Yard* (BBC), closely followed by *Dixon of Dock Green* (BBC, 1955–76).
1957–67	First hospital 'continuous serial' (soap-like): *Emergency Ward 10* (ITV).
1950–51	First children's serial: *Little Women* (BBC).

1952	A notable early classic serial was *Pride and Prejudice* (BBC). Peter Cushing played Mr Darcy, the Colin Firth role popular with the Bridget Joneses of the 1990s.
1953	First sci-fi series: *Quatermass* (BBC), produced by the innovative Rudolph Cartier, who made TV drama more televisual and produced the landmark futuristic drama *1984* (BBC, 1954), with Peter Cushing, a future Doctor Who, in the lead role.
1954	First soap opera: *The Grove Family* (BBC 1954-57).
1955	ITV, independent television, dependent on advertising for its revenue, starts broadcasting, introducing competition with the BBC, a public service broadcaster.
	ITV introduce popular dramas to attract new, ie, working class audiences not catered for by the BBC. These included *The Adventures of Robin Hood* (1955-59), sold to America even before its first broadcast and establishing a pattern of overseas sales, *Dragnet* (1955) and *Highway Patrol* (1956) and single plays with a sense of working class realism like Ted Willis's *Woman in a Dressing Gown* (1956).
1963	The BBC is now competing more successfully with ITV. Three drama sections are created under Sidney Newman, who had been brought to the BBC from ITV: serials, series and single plays. Sidney Newman commissions *Doctor Who*, which ran between 1963 and 1989, before being resurrected in 2005.
1964	BBC2 starts broadcasting.
1967	Classic drama, a literary adaptation, *The Forsyte Saga*, is broadcast in 1967 to attract viewers to BBC2. The first notable television heritage export (it sold to 45 countries for £165 million). Fantasy series like *The Saint*, *The Avengers* and *The Prisoner* (all ITV) reach younger audiences and sell well abroad. The importance of selling TV programmes (to the US, in particular), dating back to *Robin Hood* in the 1950s, becomes clear.
1970s	The single drama flourishes alongside series drama. (While series drama dominated in 1990s, the single drama is due to be revived by the BBC in 2007.)
	Some key dramas:
	1972 *War and Peace* (BBC)
	1975–1978 *The Sweeney* (ITV)
	1976 Howard Schuman's *Rock Follies* (ITV)
	1977 Mike Leigh's *Abigail's Party* (BBC)
	1978 Dennis Potter's *Pennies from Heaven* (BBC)
1980s	The single play is gradually replaced by drama series. Crime and thriller series become more popular. Lynda La Plante gives the crime genre a gender accent with *Widows* (ITV, 1983), a trend echoed in other dramas which she will continue in the 1990s.

| 1982 | Channel 4 starts broadcasting. With it, the first smaller-scale independent producers are established. |

Some key dramas:
1981 *Brideshead Revisited* (ITV) – projecting an image of heritage Britain?
1982 Alan Bleasdale's *The Boys from the Blackstuff* (BBC) – developed from a single play into a 'series' of six highly innovative televisual plays.
1984 *Jewel in the Crown* (ITV)
1984 Casualty first broadcast (BBC)
1984 *Heimat* (11-part series broadcast in subtitled format in the UK, 1985).
1985 Troy Kennedy Martin's, *Edge of Darkness* – an innovative dramatist from the 1960s, Martin wrote several *Z Cars* episodes and also scripted *The Italian Job* (US, 1969).
1986 Dennis Potter's, *The Singing Detective*.

| 1990 | Broadcasting Act demands that at least 25 percent of all major broadcasters' productions should be independently produced and that Channel 4 should become financially independent (1993). The 1990s saw the emergence of independent drama companies specialising in TV drama like Kudos and Company. BSkyB starts broadcasting (8 million subscribers by 2006). |
| 1997 | Channel 5 (later Five) starts broadcasting. |

Some key dramas:
1990 *Twin Peaks* (ABC) – the enigmatic crime/soap/supernatural hybrid.
1990 *Shoot to Kill* (ITV) – drama documentary questioning the army's alleged 'shoot to kill' policy in Northern Ireland.
1992–1994 *Between the Lines* (BBC) – challenging crime drama.
1992 *Heartbeat* – consumer-led drama (see Nelson, 1997, pp73–98).
1993 *The X-Files* (Fox Network) – sci-fi and conspiracy drama once again combine; *NYPD Blue* (ABC) hand-held camerawork becomes popularised; *Cracker* (ITV) – Jimmy McGovern's forensic psychologist drama. McGovern also wrote *Priest* (BBC, 1994), *Hillsborough* (Granada, 1996) and *The Lakes* (BBC, 1997), and most recently created the portmanteau drama *The Street* (BBC, 2006)
1994 *ER* (NBC) – first series, created by Michael Crichton, writer of *Coma* (US, 1977) and *Jurassic Park* (US, 1993). *Middlemarch* (BBC) (see Nelson, 1997, pp125–157).
1995 *Pride and Prejudice* (BBC) – revives the literary adaptation; *Hollyoaks* (Channel 4) starts broadcasting in November, capitalising on the recent rise of teen dramas such as *Dawson's Creek* (Channel 4).

1996 Peter Flannery, *Our Friends in the North* (BBC) – broadcast after lengthy attempts to get it produced, a nine-part drama following the personal and political experiences of a group of characters from the 1960s to the 1990s (see Cooke, 2003, pp170-72).

1996 –1997 *This Life* (BBC) (see Cooke, 2003, pp179–185).

1997 Tony Marchant's *Holding On* – edgy drama reflecting the anxieties inherent in city living.

1998 Tony Garnett's *The Cops* (BBC) – blending a documentary look with crime and social issues.

1999 *Warriors* (BBC) – an attempt to reflect on the ethnic conflict in Bosnia; *The West Wing* (NBC) – a positive image of US politics? Stephen Poliakoff, *Shooting the Past* (BBC).

1999-2000 Russell T Davies' *Queer as Folk* (Channel 4) – (see Creeber, 2004, pp113–155, where *Sex and the City* (1998–2004) and *This Life* are also discussed.)

1999-2004 *The Sopranos* (HBO) – (see Creeber, 2004, pp100–112).

2000s	Continuing investment in a range of drama, leading to increased confidence in genre by 2005.
2001	BBC attracts a higher audience share than ITV for the first time. *24* (Fox Network), the first of a number of 'high-concept' TV dramas, using enigma and suspense to attract viewers.
2003	Merger of Carlton and Granada. All3Media is a by-product of this rationalisation.
	Drama becomes significant for the emerging digital channels: BBC uses a digital channel (first broadcast, 2003) to experiment with new drama commissions (eg, *Casanova*, *Funland*, *Conviction*); first broadcasting in 2002, BBC4's profile increased with the dramatisation of *The Alan Clarke Diaries* (2003). ITV3, dedicated to drama, launched with *Rebus* (2004), E4 with *Friends* (2001) and More4 with *A Very Social Secretary* (2005). The switch-over to digital broadcasting is currently scheduled for 2012. Multichannel viewing (satellite and 'freeview') become more established as the decade progresses.
2004	*Desperate Housewives* (ABC) gives the 'high concept' TV a gender accent; *Lost* (ABC) is set to keep audiences in suspense for at least five series.
	Experiments with interactive drama (*Casualty*, BBC).
2005	Television on mobile phones – consumer research pilots are undertaken by the industry. The teen drama *Totally Frank* (Channel 4 and E4) shoots 13 separate mobisodes a trend now echoed with several dramas. *Lost* and *Desperate Housewives* are made available as mobisode.

2006   Sky exploits convergence to offer satellite TV, telephony, broadband and on-demand services; on-demand television.

ITV declares its commitment to original drama to compete with the BBC; Channel 4 also talks in terms of a higher profile for drama; Five continues to make significant US drama acquisitions (*CSI, House, Grey's Anatomy*) and even commissions productions (eg, drama loosely based on *Hell's Kitchen*) indicating its sense of the rise in demand for the genre.

2007   BBC to reintroduce the single play as a separate strand.

Some key dramas:

2000 Paul Abbott, *Clocking Off* (BBC) – portmanteau drama, 'ruthlessly cut to give pace' (Abbott).

2001 *Six Feet Under* (HBO) (UK: 2002, E4 and Channel 4), *24* (Fox Network) (UK: 2002, BBC).

2002 *Tipping the Velvet* (BBC); Paul Greengrass' *Bloody Sunday* (ITV); First series of *Spooks* (BBC), produced by Kudos, who later also produced *Hustle* (2004), *Life on Mars* (2006) and *The Amazing Mrs Pritchard* (2006) for the BBC.

2003 Paul Abbott, *State of Play*; *The Long Firm*; *Prime Suspect 6* (gaining 10.5 million viewers); *Holy Cross*; *Passer By*; *England Expects*, *Bodies* (all BBC).

2004 *Shameless* (Channel 4); *Yasmin* (Channel 4); *North and South* (BBC); *Life Begins* (ITV) (gaining 10.45 million viewers); *House* (Fox Network) (UK: 2005, Channel 5); *Lost*: Series 1 (ABC) (UK: 2005, Channel 4) (creator JJ Abrams also responsible for *Six Degrees*).

2005 *Rome* (HBO and BBC – second and final series 2007); the series of Shakespeare updates by the BBC, eg, *Much Ado about Nothing* and *Macbeth*; *Doctor Who* (BBC) – re-launched with unprecedented publicity; *Bleak House* (BBC) – innovative literary adaptation, also marketed and promoted strongly; new medical drama, *Grey's Anatomy* (ABC) (UK: 2006, Five).

2006 *The Street* (BBC); *Jane Eyre* (BBC); *Low Winter Sun* (Channel 4); *Robin Hood* (BBC); *Bradford Riots* (Channel 4).

Key concepts

- Genre
- Narrative
- Realism
- Representation
- Ideology
- Institution (production, distribution and exhibition contexts)
- Audience (incorporated in each of the above sections).

Applied to a drama such as *Bodies* (Hat Trick for the BBC, 2003–05 – originally broadcast on BBC3 and then moved to BBC2) these concepts can be elaborated as follows:

Genre
- Medical drama, a common subgenre of TV drama established in the late 1950s with series such as *Dr Kildare* and *Emergency Ward 10*.
- *Casualty*, its various spin-offs (*Holby City* (BBC)) and *ER* provide conventional comparisons. *Bodies* arguably alternative by comparison, with subtle variations on what audiences expect both in stylistic features (camerawork) and in its subject matter (medical incompetence leading to fatality).
- Incorporates all the standard conventions, fulfilling audience expectations of medical dramas: it combines clinical practice with potential melodrama through narratives based on doctors dealing with life-and-death situations and hospital relationships.
- Alternative and challenging narrative features (the first episode involves a death and medical errors) while the whole series is anchored on tensions between a personable but not completely competent senior consultant and his registrar, with much attention paid to the role of a ruthless and pressurising management).
- Alternative – contemporary handheld and stylised camerawork, with exaggeratedly extreme close-ups, is combined with familiar *mise en scène*, mainly restricted to hospital locations, although with a signal trademark motif (security door shot).

Narrative
- Fast-paced, elliptical, challenging.
- Series form, flexi-narrative approach.
- Character roles (mainly function but some psychological complexity).
- Positioning audiences through character and narrative structure.
- Conveying ideologies (structures of narratives – unconventional resolutions/binary oppositions).
- Narrative structures based on causal links, reinforcing the idea of logic, a belief in causation.

Realism

- Characters and narratives which are plausible – help to convince audiences and provide the effect of reality.
- *Mise en scène* designed to look realistic (appropriate sets, locations, dress and lighting).
- Camerawork – although stylised and contemporary, aimed at conveying realism
- Sound – mainly diegetic but non-diegetic sound is not intrusive.

Representation

In particular:

- Gender.
- Ethnicity.
- NHS and the hospital management.
- Challenging and questioning.

Institution

- Independent production company, Hat Trick (producers of *Have I Got News for You* but branching out into drama), *Bodies* was produced for the BBC to a budget. (Following the 1990 Broadcasting Act, the BBC were required to commission 25 percent of its scheduled programming from outside the corporation.)
- Produced for the new digital channel, BBC3 (for which a signficant amount of new drama has been commissioned). Subsequently broadcast on BBC2, with the following episode broadcast immediately afterwards on BBC3 (a common recent scheduling practice to attract viewers to digital channels) – TV drama's role in promoting and sustaining digital TV channels.
- Scripted by former doctor Jed Mercurio, whose previous fast-paced and challenging *Cardiac Arrest* (Channel 4, 1994) also raised issues about the running of the NHS (notably its creeping privatisation).

Audience

- Targeting a knowledgeable audience, appealing to leftwing sensibilities; also aiming to attract a younger audience by using fast-paced narrative and camerawork (17–34 sector).
- Differential readings possible.

These are the kinds of issues you will be raising with your students when dealing with an average TV drama. It is important, therefore, to start by exploring in more detail the key media concepts that inform them.

First principles: constructions

Most TV drama attempts to convince audiences of its realism. In order to create the *effect* of the real world, all media has to be constructed. It is a familiar concept to all media teachers: that the media deals not with a 'window on the world' but is a constructed representation of it. The media is constructed in two obvious senses: first, it is literally constructed using for example sets, costume, lighting, camerawork and editing; second, it is metaphorically 'constructed' to create the illusion of reality. When studying a media product like a TV drama, you are therefore exploring how it is constructed (in terms of genre, narrative and representation), what influences its construction (eg, production and broadcasting contexts) and what impact the construction will have on audiences. In other words, TV dramas are shaped by the institutions which produce and broadcast them as well as by the audiences they aim to attract.

● Genre

In studying genre, students generally uncover:
- How genres are constructed: combining repeated motifs, which become conventions and thus act like codes, with slight variations on them;
- How audiences seem to like this combination of fulfilled generic expectations with slight variations, playing against expectations;
- How genres balance industry and audience needs;
- How genres are therefore dynamic and flexible, open to change, to suit both industry and audiences;
- How far today's genres veer towards hybrids – or have they always done?
- How genres tend to reflect and reinforce the dominant ideologies of contemporary society, thus *tending* to the conservative;
- How genres can, nevertheless, be a means of raising social issues and challenging dominant ideologies (as with *Bodies*).

How the idea of genre developed

Genre literally means 'kind' or 'type' (from the Latin word 'genus') and thus describes a particular category of television programme or film. With the development of publishing, most obviously in the mass-market publishing of the 19th century, genre played an important role in reaching a mass audience. So although genre indicates much about audience preferences, its commercial significance lies in its role of attracting audiences to media products.

As far as television and film are concerned, this commercial idea of genre grew with the evolution of the film industry but was particularly developed in Hollywood in the 1920s and 1930s, when the major film studios were being established as vertically integrated companies. Film producers wanted ways of attracting audiences to their films in order to create profit. The obvious solution was to establish what kinds of film people liked and produce large numbers of them. Marketers could thus give films a label (eg, melodrama, Western or gangster) so that audiences knew what to expect, thereby luring them into the cinema. Genres thus became formulas consisting of predictable ingredients audiences liked.

A central purpose of genre is to reach mass audiences – ensuring audience appeal and financial profit. What film, radio and subsequently television producers built into their genres was a response to what they thought audiences wanted; if audiences turned away from a particular version of the genre, producers modified it. Genres have therefore always been open to modification. For audiences, the appeal of genre products seems to be in the expectations they fulfil, while at the same time playing against them. Genres thus provide a mixture of repeated elements with slight variations. The principle that genres comprise dynamic rather than fixed conventions, which balance producers' (commercial) needs with audiences' interests, was thus established early in the history of media production. The question underlying all study of a genre like TV drama is therefore how far broadcasters' needs and audience interests affect the nature of the drama itself.

Worksheet 1: Thinking about genre

1 of 2 pages

To access student worksheets and other online materials go to *Teaching TV Drama* at **www.bfi.org.uk/tfms** and enter User name: **tvdrama@bfi.org.uk** and Password: **te0310dr**.

Establishing what TV drama is

What audiences and broadcasters past and present have understood by TV drama has varied; and whether audiences and broadcasters today think of TV drama in the same way is debatable. It is thus an important starting point to establish a provisional definition for classroom use.

Worksheet 2: What is TV drama?

1 of 2 pages

Listing examples of soap opera, crime drama, costume drama, plays, mini-series, series drama, teen drama demonstrates the distinction between TV drama as an overall genre and its various subgenres, 'genres within genres'. It should also draw attention to the different forms TV drama may take: one-off dramas, dramas in two parts and the various 'long-form' dramas (to use Glen Creeber's term) like drama series, drama serials and continuing dramas (soap operas). Some students may build in the kind of value judgements mentioned in Section 1, which regard single dramas, classic literary adaptations and some drama series as 'drama' and soaps as an inferior category, which is not genuine drama at all. On the very edge of the genre is drama-documentary – a hybrid and best treated separately in my opinion. Some drama-documentaries are dramas attempting to reconstruct events, such as the landmark *Shoot to Kill* (ITV, 1990), whereas more recently there has been a tendency to emphasise the fictional, dramatic elements and use a real event as the background, such as *Bradford Riots* (Channel 4, 2006). A working definition for TV drama can thus be established (noted in Section 1): fictionalised action in narrative form produced for television (a definition which captures the root meaning of the word 'drama'). Even more simply, TV drama is a fictional television narrative.

Basic conventions of TV drama

By looking at extracts from three or more contrasting TV dramas, students should be able to establish that the basic conventions of TV drama revolve around:

- Characters
- Narrative – both its characteristic structures and how it is constructed in visual terms
- Sets and settings (the basic elements of *mise en scène*)
- Camerawork
- Dialogue, sound and music

Worksheet 3: TV drama conventions 1

worksheet 3 **TV drama conventions 1**

The conventions of a genre are the ingredients which all examples of a genre share. They act a little like rules – not necessarily rigid rules but rules you need to follow in order to create something which audiences will recognise as part of a particular genre. Like other conventions – governing speech and behaviour, for example – audiences seem to assimilate the conventions of genres unconsciously.

Establishing the conventions of TV drama

Choose three or four contrasting TV dramas and look at short extracts from them. Here are some suggestions: a single drama like *Yasmin*, a crime or medical series like *The Shield* or *Green Wing*, a US drama series like *24* (2001), *Lost* or *Desperate Housewives*, a drama serial like the classic literary adaptation *Bleak House* (2005), a sensational drama like *Footballers' Wives* or a teen drama like *The OC*.

What is different about the drama series *24*? Did it establish a new trend?

Page 1 of 2   TV Drama

1 of 2 pages

To access student worksheets and other online materials go to *Teaching TV Drama* at **www.bfi.org.uk/tfms** and enter User name: **tvdrama@bfi.org.uk** and Password: **te0310dr**.

Any study of TV drama will always involve examining how these conventions are used by producers and perceived by audiences. In exploring a series of extracts, the ideas underpinning key concepts and some theoretical perspectives will emerge:

- Character roles (possibly some basic reference to Propp) and oppositions (Lévi-Strauss); representational issues
- How narratives are constructed (role of editing, audience positioning, the relevance of Tzvetan Todorov's claims about narrative to TV drama and Robin Nelson's idea of 'flexi-narrative');
- The way *mise en scène* is created (its connotations);
- Generic dialogue, music and sound;
- Icons of particular subgenres;
- Institutional issues – the significance of TV drama to broadcasting organisations;
- Audience issues.

Worksheet 4: TV drama conventions 2

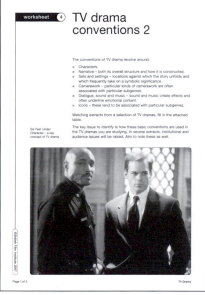

1 of 2 pages

To access student worksheets and other online materials go to *Teaching TV Drama* at **www.bfi.org.uk/tfms** and enter User name: **tvdrama@bfi.org.uk** and Password: **te0310dr**.

Characters

Characters are clearly a crucial element of TV drama. Many dramas are defined by the lead character or groups of characters acting together or as teams: *Morse, Frost, Taggart, Monk, Cagney and Lacey, Ultimate Force, Footballers' Wives, Murder Investigation Team.* The common ingredient is that audiences are being invited to identify with the lead characters and are interested in what happens to them. However, audiences may actually relate to characters in more general ways.

Footballers' Wives

The tendency is to assume that audience interest in characters arises from gradually understanding how they think and feel, their psychological make-up and what motivates them. Although this is undeniably partly the case, many dramas seem to encourage audiences to respond to characters in more fundamental ways. The desire to see happy endings, with the 'good' characters triumphing over the 'bad', arguably takes over from individual characterisation. In other words, audiences see TV drama characters in terms of roles.

Most teen dramas – like *Charmed* (Five), *The OC* (Channel 4), *Buffy the Vampire Slayer* (BBC), *Smallville* (Channel 4) – are based on adolescent concerns. The desire for relationships, the problems arising from them, the desire to be individual if not special, equated with powers which will idealistically solve other people's problems and cast individuals in the role of hero, all feature strongly. Characters tend to conform to fantasy roles, which are played out in different contexts. *Pride and Prejudice*, Andrew Davies's literary adaptation from 1995 which has reached almost legendary status, is fundamentally predicated on the audience's desire for the central characters, Elizabeth (prejudiced) and Darcy (proud), to love and live happily ever after. Indeed, most viewers know that this will happen and derive pleasure from seeing it enacted.

In *Footballers' Wives*, most audiences quickly recognise Tanya Turner or Eva Da Wolfe as the calculating schemers they are both (knowingly) portrayed as. Both play an obvious gender role, shocking audiences by their ability to exploit people through their sexuality. Viewers want to see whether either one of them is going to get away with it rather than ask questions about the possible psychological roots of their motivation. Audiences are effectively, and possibly unconsciously, debating whether or not women are entitled to exercise power in terms of their sexuality.

Viewers therefore appear to respond most to the role which characters play rather than their psychological make-up. This is one of the ideas underlying Vladimir Propp's claims about narrative which emerged from his study into the characteristics and structures of fairy tales, *The Morphology of the Fairy Tale* (originally written in 1928). His claim that characters' narrative function is more important than their psychological identity does hint at the dominant way TV drama is experienced by most audiences. Gill Branston and Roy Stafford put it like this:

> [Vladimir Propp's theory] reminds us that, though characters in stories may seem very 'real', especially in cinema and television, they must be understood as constructed characters, who have roles to play for the sake of the story and so often get perceived very quickly as 'hero', 'villain', 'helper' and so on with many accompanying expectations.
> (Branston and Stafford, 2006, p25)

(A more detailed discussion of Propp's central ideas is included in Nick Lacey's *Narrative and* Genre, 2000, pp46–64.

The most basic of these roles is the polarisation of characters into 'good' and 'bad'. The majority of narratives involve characters who are in conflict with one another. Many set up conflicts between good and bad characters and build the narrative around revealing how good will triumph over bad. This is clearly what informs Lévi-Strauss's idea of binary opposition: narratives are frequently organised in terms of characters, ideas and values which are set in opposition to one another. These tend to be categorised by audiences as either good or bad. The narrative standardly resolves this opposition in favour of the good. Lévi-Strauss pointed out that this was an almost 'mythical' resolution in that it suggested such outcomes were possible in narratives in the way they were not in real life.

Crucially, this suggests that characters are deeply embedded in narratives. And it also points to the way audiences are constantly being positioned to sympathise with some characters (and the values and attitudes they represent) and be antagonistic to others (and the values and attitudes they represent). Audiences' attitudes, values and beliefs are thus being shaped by their involvement in narratives.

Worksheet 5: Working with characters

1 of 2 pages

To access student worksheets and other online materials go to *Teaching TV Drama* at **www.bfi.org.uk/tfms** and enter User name: **tvdrama@bfi.org.uk** and Password: **te0310dr**.

Generic narratives

Studying TV drama narratives involves recognising how they are constructed to position audiences and how they are structured according to their form (which obviously varies depending on whether the drama is a serial, a series or a self-contained single drama). However, most TV drama and its various sub-genres have particular kinds of narratives associated with them. Soap operas and medical dramas (arguably female-oriented) tend to emphasise reflection and relationships; medical dramas in general combine that with narratives based on the treatment of patients (generally successful but with token failures); police/crime dramas are based on crime and investigation, generally concluding with the successful capture of criminals; teen dramas dramatise adolescent issues, with idealised solutions. Most employ settings, characters and issues that appeal to mainstream audiences – gender, ethnicity, the police, hospitals and schools, for example.

Mise en scène, *camerawork, dialogue/sound and music*

Equally significant to the way audiences respond to, and make sense of, TV dramas is the way other generic conventions are used – notably *mise en scène*, camerawork and sound, dialogue and music. Generally speaking, they draw in viewers and emphasise aspects of character and narrative. In other words, they are part of a positioning process.

Mise en scène

The main elements of *mise en scène* include sets and locations, lighting and costume and it is a significant component in creating realism. However, it also positions audiences by instantly conveying ideas and points of view.

Exploring it reveals the following:
- The connotations of *mise en scène* suggest ideas to audiences, underlining narrative and representational issues;
- Departures from conventional *mise en scène* add significance and appeal for audiences;
- *Mise en scène* is frequently used as a way of marketing dramas, particularly costume dramas, as a guarantee of the quality of the production (the financial resources deployed in order to establish realism – note *Radio Times* features 'Getting Behind the Scenes').

Connotations underline narrative and representational issues: The desert island setting in *Lost* – at first apparently paradisical – suggests isolation, danger and threat, and the need for resourcefulness. It represents an opportunity to observe a society where the trappings of civilisation are taken away and new ways of behaving persist. It becomes the place where human values can be reconsidered and redefined. Audiences may relate this to films like *Lord of the Flies* (either Harry Hook's (1990) or Peter Brook's (1963) film version) or to the recent survival dramas like *The Edge* (1997) or *Cast Away* (2000). But most obviously, following the idea for the drama (using the reality TV show formula of characters put in extreme positions where they have to carry out tasks, like *I'm a Celebrity, Get Me Out of Here*), audiences are likely to view this in relation to a range of possible genres. The power of the drama's central narrative enigma is that it can draw on so many different genres (horror, sci-fi, conspiracy, game/reality show). The *mise en scène* of dramas like *Footballers' Wives* and *Desperate Housewives* underline the gender representations in both series as well as obviously exposing the superficiality of the material worlds the characters inhabit.

Intertextual significance – the postmodern touch: The sense that audiences may respond to *Lost* in a way mediated by contemporary television culture is arguably not dissimilar to dramas like *Doctor Who* on the one hand or the overtly hybrid Peter Bowker drama *Blackpool* (2004) on the other. Episode 2 of the 2005 series of *Doctor Who*, 'The End of the World' (scripted by series creator Russell T Davies) has a space station platform to witness the 'End of the World' (Justin Richards, pp58-69). The stage set, which includes a variety of aliens, juxtaposes the Doctor and Rose in a way intended to allow audiences to identify with them. One alien, Cassandra, turns out to be the saboteur among the assembled crowd. What are the connotations of her 'construction', comprising stretched skin, a brain in a designer jar and attendants who moisturise the skin? Audiences see the ultimate in cosmetic surgery – which Davies saw as a parodic allusion to *Nip/Tuck* (2003) – a hideous skin who/which has had 708 operations. And later in the episode, the Doctor must pass over a bridge-like structure to reach the device which will raise the shield and prevent the space platform from being destroyed with the end of the world! The narrative, as well as the setting, suggests the world of computer games – a contemporary, mediated way of relating to the sets and costumes of *Doctor Who*. *Blackpool* uses the connotations of seediness and superficial glitz to take us into a world of duplicitous glamour and shady dealings in a drama which also incorporates musical numbers in the fashion of Dennis Potter.

Compared with the more conventional use of *mise en scène* in *ER* and *Bodies*, the recent US drama *House* provides a subtle variation on convention. Set in a research hospital, the environment is predominantly light, with supposedly state-of-the art facilities and considerable time is spent in a room and lab associated with the research team. Audiences interpret this as slightly unconventional and it thus provides a fresh take on medical drama (accentuating the challenging representation of medicine as an uncertain experimental path towards diagnosis and embodied by the dominant and cantankerous House, who nevertheless heroically manages to solve all problems with dazzling displays of rational acumen). The drama thus inconspicuously combines the medical with the investigative problem-solving narratives of crime dramas.

Classic dramas, such as the recent adaptation of *Bleak House*, the now near-iconic 1995 *Pride and Prejudice* or Chorion's *Poirot* and *Miss Marple* for ITV, demonstrate a conventional use of *mise en scène* by painstakingly meticulous reconstructions of the past, expected by audiences and exploited by promoters. The recent *Life on Mars* exemplified programming based on the nostalgia exploited in the drama (BBC4's 1970s week, shown around a re-run of the series on the digital channel).

Camerawork

TV drama is most often associated with establishing shots, shot-reverse shot, medium close-up and close-up for emotional moments. Just as soap operas allow themselves more dramatic camerawork at intense moments, many TV dramas employ the production values and camerawork associated with film. *Messiah* is an interesting case in point. It uses the highly stylised range of camerawork associated with film production values, not to mention the explicit references to David Fincher's *Seven* (1995); while Channel 4's *Ghost Squad* relies on predominantly handheld camerawork and pans rather than cuts to inject pace – a characteristic of several dramas since the innovative *NYPD Blue* first popularised this technique in the early 1990s.

Sound

Sound, whether diegetic (an integral part of the narrative) or non-diegetic (not part of the framework of the narrative, such as 'background' music), is used most significantly to punctuate action, create effects such as suspense and tension, and underline emotional moments. Non-diegetic music in particular is now a conventional aspect of TV drama, whereas even in the early 1980s it was much less common for dramas to feature a significant amount of music.

Worksheet 6: TV drama conventions 3

1 of 2 pages

To access student worksheets and other online materials go to *Teaching TV Drama* at **www.bfi.org.uk/tfms** and enter User name: **tvdrama@bfi.org.uk** and Password: **te0310dr**.

Modifications to the genre

As a balance between industry and audience needs, genres are always open to modification, albeit within certain limits. Looking at police drama we can quickly see how the genre's use of investigating characters has altered, reflecting changes in society. The avuncular 'bobby on the beat' from *Dixon of Dock Green* in the 1950s turned into the partnership of *Z Cars* (a formula which has permeated several crime dramas since – eg, *The Sweeney*, *Hill Street Blues*, *Cagney and Lacey*, *Starsky and Hutch* and *Homicide*). Female partnerships emerged in the later 1970s and 1980s (*Cagney and Lacey*, *Juliet Bravo*, *Prime Suspect*, *Linda Lee*). Forensic scientists and crime scene investigators appeared in the 1990s (*Silent Witness* and *CSI*). More recently cold case investigators and specialist teams have provided another variation on the investigating figure: *Waking the Dead*, *New Tricks* and *Rosemary and Thyme* also gave roles to more mature people, capitalising on their experience; while *The Shield* and *Ghost Squad* provided yet another variation on the investigating team, both of which use unconventional methods to clear up crime. *Cracker* in the 1990s, and the more recent *Wire in the Blood,* foregrounded forensic psychologists as investigator, while undercover police are at the centre of the recent *Murphy's Law*.

Each drama tends to reflect the dominant ideologies of the society at the time it was made. *Dixon* reflected the sense of confidence people had in the police force in the 1950s, where audiences were convinced by the morals with which Dixon concluded his story. In the 1960s, *Z Cars* demonstrated that the police were human too, while *The Sweeney*, following several police corruption cases of the 1960s and early 1970s, gave voice to the view that the police worked at the very edge of the law. More recently, police investigations have been portrayed as relying on procedure, reflecting the demand that the police be accountable, work within the law and rely on sophisticated information support to secure convictions. There is not so much absolute justice as a relativised justice within the confines of the legal system.

Modifications in the genre of TV drama can also be seen in the way hybrids are constantly being created. Arguably, they always have been (as Rick Altman points out in his provocative *Film/Genre*, on genre in relation to the film industry). Again, crime is a good example: there are overt hybrids such as Dennis Potter's combination of psychological drama, noir-like investigators and musical, more recently replicated in Peter Bowker's *Blackpool* (earlier versions included Steve Bochco's *Rock Follies*, 1976). The mixture of the psychological with crime drama, echoing Christopher Norris's film *Memento* (2000), emerged in a spate of ITV dramas which all featured memory loss; *Messiah*, following *Seven*, combined serial killer investigative crime with the spectacle of horror; *Hustle* combined action, comedy and avenging crime; *Sea of Souls* and *Murder Prevention* both blended sci- fi with crime conventions.

Even more obviously, teen dramas such as *Buffy the Vampire Slayer* (and its various offshoots) combined horror with teen drama, whereas *Charmed* mixed supernatural magic, comedy and teen drama, and *Doctor Who* blended sci-fi, comedy (through conscious self-parody) and intertextual references to the world of computer gaming. *Footballers' Wives* and *Cutting It* heighten the melodrama of soap opera into the sensational and the sexual. This kind of hybrid, as with *Doctor Who*, seems to promote a different kind of audience response – a postmodern reaction in keeping with contemporary ideologies, where audiences revel in the drama's extremes at the same time as being fully aware of its artificiality.

Worksheet 7: Genre – Open to change

1 of 2 pages

To access student worksheets and other online materials go to *Teaching TV Drama* at **www.bfi.org.uk/tfms** and enter User name: **tvdrama@bfi.org.uk** and Password: **te0310dr**.

Challenging dominant ideologies

There have been signal dramas from the past – like Alan Bleasdale's 1982 *Boys from the Blackstuff* – which have challenged the dominant ideologies of the time by focusing dramatically on contemporary social issues (like unemployment in the grotesquely comic and harrowing 'Yosser's Story'). Whether it is true that TV drama today is less politicised, as is sometimes claimed, there are certainly notable examples of dramas which use the genre to challenge dominant ideologies. Russell T Davies's *Queer as Folk*, in revelling in and celebrating all aspects of contemporary gay culture, did just that, as did *Six Feet Under* in its challenging representation of several aspects of identity politics. Paul Abbott's *State of Play* attempted to offer some sense of political questioning (although not quite as radically as past dramas like *Edge of*

Darkness or the drama-documentary *Shoot to Kill*); Abi Morgan's *Sex Traffic* and Simon Beaufoy's *Yasmin* both raised important social and political issues; and *Shameless*, in often painfully grotesque ways, has uncovered aspects of social class in Britain today which are both challenging and humorous at the same time.

Worksheet 8: Challenging dramas

To access student worksheets and other online materials go to *Teaching TV Drama* at **www.bfi.org.uk/tfms** and enter User name: **tvdrama@bfi.org.uk** and Password: **te0310dr**.

1 of 2 pages

Conclusion

What this approach to genre suggests is that the categorising aspects of genre study are less important than how broadcasters and audiences 'use' genres. This section has drawn attention to how issues can be raised through genre and how audiences can respond as much to those issues as to the generic conventions which frame them. Nevertheless, the nature of a drama, particularly the way in which people and issues are represented, is shaped by broadcasters' and producers' awareness of genre and audience.

● Narrative

Narrative is fundamental to the study of media, as it underlies all genres in all media forms. Narratives can be pleasurable, accessible and entertaining; they are also part of people's everyday lives. We are surrounded by narratives and arguably relate to one another and to the media in terms of narrative. Narratives are consequently powerful: they suggest ideas and raise issues. They thus become one of the central ways through which people assimilate points of view, attitudes, values and beliefs without even realising it. Crucially, they also reinforce a belief in cause and effect and the idea that there are rational explanations which can account for human behaviour. Narratives shape *how* people think and feel – in terms of narrative and the principles informing it – as well as *what* people think and feel – the values, attitudes and beliefs individuals come to hold and which, in turn, they use to perceive the world. TV drama narratives are, thus, always more than mere stories.

In order to understand these ideas, this section explores:
- how TV drama narratives are constructed from a series of selected images;
- how these narratives as a whole are structured (the subject of several theories, which this section will attempt to integrate in its approach).

What is a narrative?

At their simplest, media narratives, whether in the form of TV drama, film or documentaries, are stories told in images. How the images are selected and pieced together determines the nature of the narrative.

You could take any simple sequence of images to demonstrate this, such as an extract from *Lost* (Series 1/Episode 4, 10:33–11:36). This sequence tells a simple story: a black American asks a reserved Korean woman to look after his son while he goes into the jungle. But what it also demonstrates is a sense of humanity, that people divided by nationality and culture are all capable of helping one another. It similarly gives a positive view of both the black American man and the Korean woman, who takes on the role of a mother. Both provide positive representations of their respective cultures.

The individual shots and the way they are juxtaposed (the camerawork, *mise en scène* and editing) do not simply underline these points: they are the means by which audiences recognise them. For the way this narrative is presented to them encourages audiences to react in a particular way: to be sympathetic to both the American man and the Korean woman, and to respond to the simple act of human kindness underlying it. The narrative encourages audiences to take up a particular point of view – it positions them (in the words of Stuart Hall). This does not of course mean that all audiences will adopt the same position – there will be those who combine their own views with what they are being encouraged to think (negotiated readings) and those who reject what is being suggested (oppositional readings). However, narratives are structured in such a way that audiences have to take a position; they adopt points of view based on what they have seen.

What audiences also do is relate this fragment of a narrative to other elements of the narrative – in this case, within the overarching narrative of the series. The significance of the narrative is thus enhanced, when we realise that the Korean woman is confined within some kind of oppressive, patriarchal relationship (at this stage we are uncertain what it is). In an earlier incident, the Korean man she is with tells her sternly to do up the top button of her cardigan in the presence of this same black American; later on, she undoes the button with a sense of defiance and independence that audiences are positioned to approve of. In another incident, the black American pretends to have found his son's Labrador, omitting to mention, however, that it was actually another character who found the dog. This scene adds another layer to this narrative strand.

Additional significance is provided, then, by relating this narrative moment to other elements in the series. So narratives never simply tell stories – they communicate points of view about what is being shown. The point of view may be explicit, as in a first-person voiceover narration (in films such as *Goodfellas* (1990), *LA Confidential* (1997) and numerous film noirs or TV dramas like *Tipping the Velvet* and *Desperate Housewives*); or it may be implicit, concealed within the more conventional third-person narrative. This links with the root meaning of the word 'narrative', which comes from the idea of 'knowing'. Hence, 'narrative' implies someone who knows something and communicates it to others.

Narratives are always selective: they never provide audiences with all the background. Victor Shlovsky, in the 1920s, pointed this out when he distinguished between the narrative as it is presented to audiences (the plot/*suzhet*) and the details audiences assume – the implied backstory or details which it is not necessary to show (the story/*fabula*). The significant point is, however, ideological: as a result of selecting key images, juxtaposing them in a sequence and using particular camera shots, lighting, dialogue and music, audiences are being positioned.

Worksheet 9: Narrative construction

To access student worksheets and other online materials go to *Teaching TV Drama* at **www.bfi.org.uk/tfms** and enter User name: **tvdrama@bfi.org.uk** and Password: **te0310dr**.

1 of 2 pages

Conventions of narratives

The ingredients of narratives can be explored in several ways. You can present stories in different ways; you can use contrasting kinds of story like an advertisement, a news item and a cartoon; you can use prediction exercises; or you can use fairy tales. (Mark Readman explores this kind of approach in his book in this series.) **Worksheet 9: Narrative construction** uses a story based on the episode from *Spooks* considered in Case Study 3.

By asking about the common ingredients of narrative – narrative conventions – several points, including the narrative theories with which they are often associated, should emerge. For example:

- Narratives have structures: beginnings, middles and endings (Aristotle and Todorov) although serialised TV dramas (whether continuous drama series – soaps – or dramatised serialisations, like classic drama) exhibit a variation on that closed structure.
- Narratives do not tell us everything – they are selective. There is a difference between the narrative as it is structured for audiences in a TV drama and the complete backstory to the characters (Shlovsky's distinction between *suzhet* and *fibula*, already mentioned).
- They introduce us to characters and create a narrative based on those characters (Aristotle and Propp).
- They often have good and bad characters (Propp and Lévi-Strauss).
- They are designed to involve audiences and make them sympathise with some characters rather than others (Aristotle and Barthes).
- They often have multiple storylines (Robin Nelson's 'flexi-narrative'), a structure originally associated with soap opera but which now underlies much contemporary TV drama, particularly mainstream TV drama.

Most of these conventions relate to the structure of narratives generally. TV narratives employ many of them but also have some distinctive features.

Narrative structures and generic forms

Narrative structures are either open or closed: closed narratives have beginnings, middles and endings (Aristotle's view), or narrative equilibrium, disequilibrium and restoration of equilibrium (Todorov's view); open narratives either never reach a clear conclusion or end ambiguously. TV drama has ranged from closed narratives like single dramas and open narratives like soap operas. But of course much TV drama combines the two: the 'flexi-narrative' of drama series combines open narratives – storylines (narrative arcs) which follow different characters across several episodes – with closed narratives (each episode is self-contained and reaches a conclusion). Similarly, the serial has the openness of soap opera (often concluding with soap opera's suspenseful 'cliffhanger', knowingly accentuated in Andrew Davies's *Bleak House*, BBC, 2005) as well as the closed narrative of single drama, in that it reaches a conclusion over its total number of episodes.

However, whether narratives are open or closed, it is the ideological implications of their structures which are most significant. For narratives characteristically seek to reassure audiences that whatever problems are exposed can be resolved, whether it is through individual human endeavour or society's institutions (such as law and order and the power of medicine) or (usually) a combination of the two. Abi Morgan's *Sex Traffic* (2004), a single drama shown in two parts, did exactly that. It exposed the disturbingly exploitative, savage and patriarchal world of sex trafficking. Within an essentially three-act structure, the narrative was resolved positively as the female protagonist is able to return to her native Moldova to be reunited with her son. Those behind the corrupt, private, multinational security companies, working with the connivance of United Nations officers, were satisfyingly exposed and captured.

The drama series *Doctor Who* provides an obvious example of a series where each self-contained narrative is resolved. Series 2/Episode 2 is an example of a narrative resolution through heroic, individual agency. The episode blends Victorian Gothic horror, the Gothic fantasy of *Buffy the Vampire Slayer* and martial arts combat sequences (as popularised in *The Matrix*, 1999, *Crouching Tiger, Hidden Dragon*, 2000, and *Hero*, 2002) with humorous social comment at the expense of contemporary royalty. It shows the Doctor returning to 1869, where he uses his ingenuity to defeat a werewolf bent on destroying Queen Victoria and her empire. Crime and medical dramas use the same ideological structure to reassure audiences of the effectiveness of legal and medical institutions (see Case Study 1).

Narratives in TV dramas are thus constructed to attract audiences and convince them that the world is a place where 'happy endings' are possible.

● Realism

The central issues underlying the study of realism are:

● Conventions creating the effect of the real
   - Realism consists of codes and conventions which aim to convey a sense of reality to audiences.
   - Realism comprises the *effect* of the real and is thus created by codes and conventions which refer more to other codes and conventions than reality itself. (We do not all refer to the same thing when we refer to 'reality', in any case.) What we see in the media are copies of copies (simulacra), to use Baudrillard's terms.

- Codes of realism differ and are constantly open to change
  - The codes and conventions of realism vary over time and are constantly open to change. They can be extended and modified as audience perceptions about what counts as 'realistic' change.
  - The conventions of realism vary from one culture to another – eg, Bollywood melodrama is perceived to be fundamentally realistic.
  - As new technologies are developed – such as lightweight hand-held cameras, steadicams, more sophisticated editing techniques and special effects – new conventions of realism are established.
  - Thus, a sense of reality can be conveyed in several ways. There are several forms of realism and no one form is intrinsically more realistic than another.

- Realism: an ideological version of reality
  - Realism is a version of reality, and cannot be divorced from the values, attitudes and beliefs it conveys. Realism is thus an ideological representation of reality. It might be the programme-makers' views or a point of view which they feel is commonly held (a consensual viewpoint).
  - Realism is a way of organising the real – creating a hierarchy of what is important and what's more marginal. It gives prominence to some values, attitudes and beliefs over others.

Conventions creating the effect of the real

TV drama, like the vast majority of media forms, aims to convince audiences that it provides a window on reality. It does this by using a series of conventions, which act like codes and create the 'effect' of reality (as Raymond Williams put it). So camerawork, editing, *mise en scène* (which, importantly, includes lighting and costume), characters, narratives, dialogue, sound (diegetic or non-diegetic) and particular generic icons (like medical dress, electro-shock pads for cardiac arrests) all play their role in creating this effect. These conventions frequently convince audiences that what they see corresponds with their sense of reality, but that 'sense' of reality is probably based more on other TV dramas and media than any direct experience of what is depicted (even if 'direct' experience of reality guarantees realism). Take the cardiac arrest equipment, which appears in virtually every medical drama: few viewers will have actually seen this equipment in action but they are convinced that it is 'realistic' (and it, of course, brings with it the drama of potentially reviving a patient on the operating table).

Worksheet 10: The conventions of realism

worksheet 10 **The conventions of realism**

Dramas do not provide windows on reality, but offer audiences versions of reality using codes and conventions designed to convince them of this. Realism is constructed and is essentially an effect.

To explore this, choose two contrasting hospital-based medical dramas (like *ER*, *House* and *Bodies*). How do they convey the sense of the reality of a hospital?

Think about the following:

- What kinds of characters appear and what are they wearing?
- What is the narrative about? How is it constructed?
- What are the most significant features of the mise en scène?
- What kind of camerawork is used?
- Do you notice anything particular about the editing?
- What sort of dialogue is used (any dialogue that you particularly associate with hospitals)?
- What other sound is used? Ambient (natural) sound? Music? Effects of any kind?

House: A stage managed, promotional pose. How far are all dramas constructed?

Page 1 of 2   TV Drama

1 of 2 pages

To access student worksheets and other online materials go to *Teaching TV Drama* at **www.bfi.org.uk/tfms** and enter User name: **tvdrama@bfi.org.uk** and Password: **te0310dr**.

ER, a long-running US drama, created by Michael Crichton, and *Bodies* (2003–05), a drama first shown on BBC3, a BBC digital channel, before moving to BBC2, and scripted by former doctor Jed Mercurio, writer of 1994's *Cardiac Arrest* (Channel 4), use the full range of conventions to convey a sense of reality but do so in slightly different ways. The characters and narratives conform to what we expect: the central characters include surgeons, doctors, nurses, patients and administrators; narratives revolve around clinical cases, the various backgrounds of individual patients and the lives (and relationships) of doctors and nurses. The camerawork in *ER* is characteristically fluid (a large amount of steadicam work is used, partly as a result of the studio design, which is 'hard-walled' – see Worksheet **10: The conventions of realism**) and a variety of pace in editing. Clinical dialogue is employed and narratives frequently close on a poignant, human theme, coupled with non-diegetic but evocative piano music to punctuate the narrative emotionally. *Bodies* employs more stylised camerawork – steadicam combined with handheld, extreme close-ups and a faster pace of editing. Both sets of conventions signify realism, and act on viewers like codes. Already with these two examples, the realism being conveyed is slightly different. But audiences find no difficulty in responding to them both as 'realistic'. In other words, the codes of realism (based, here, on camera, lighting and editing) are used differently but still convince audiences. There is no one code of realism, but several.

Codes of realism differ and are constantly open to change

If you compare *ER* and *Bodies* with other hospital dramas, the way in which the codes of realism can vary becomes even clearer. Take *Casualty* (BBC1, 1984–), the longest-running hospital drama produced in Britain, *No Angels* (World Productions/Channel 4, 2004), which focuses primarily on the female – and mainly sexual – perspectives of nurses, and *Grey's Anatomy* (ABC/Five, 2005–), which also foregrounds sexuality among the demands of a group of surgeon interns at a teaching hospital in Seattle. They all provide familiar, 'realistic' views of hospitals, which viewers perceive as real. However, the 'look' of reality in each drama is markedly different. *Casualty* uses predominantly studio-based camerawork and a relatively slow pace of editing; *No Angels* employs a much faster pace of editing, coupled with a lot of steadicam, hand-held camerawork and overexposed lighting to create a more artificial feel; while *Grey's Anatomy* uses the space and fluid camerawork of *ER*.

The degree to which the 'effect' of reality is convincing depends more on how successfully the codes borrow from one another than on how far they relate to the 'reality' of hospitals. To take an example from the even more popular crime genre, the forensic laboratories of *Waking the Dead* (2000–) were perceived by some audiences as less realistic mainly because they apparently didn't conform to the image audiences had of laboratories (doubtless based on *Silent Witness*, 1996–, and other crime dramas). When *CSI: NY* (2004–) introduced a forensic laboratory integrated within an office working environment, it was coded to suggest that it was a modern and efficient forensic environment. It effectively achieved this by using a *mise en scène* with connotations of technological sophistication and modernity – light environment of glass and steel, suffused with computer screens and other hi-tech devices, all of which suggested a modern image of science to audiences. And that itself conveyed a view that scientific investigation was the only way in which crimes could be solved.

Audiences know all this because they have seen it before – in other TV dramas. To think in Baudrillard's terms, the codes of realism develop from one another: they are 'simulacra', a word he reserved to indicate that all media representations were copies of previous media representations, which were themselves copies of yet other media representations, and so on. TV drama conveys its sense of realism by referring to other TV drama rather than reality itself. As Baudrillard claims, it is almost that what people assume is 'reality' is in fact a kind of 'hyperreality' – the artificial or heightened reality of the media. Media representations, including those of TV drama, dominate people's thinking so much that the world of the media becomes more real than the 'real' world. In that sense, the dominant representations in people's minds are media representations. This is parodied in different ways in the films *Being There* (1976), *The Truman Show* (1998) and *Nurse Betty* (2000), all of which force audiences to confront the conventional nature of realism.

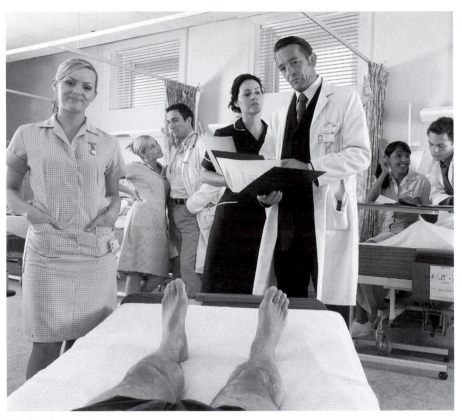

No Angels

Realism is also historically, culturally and socially relative. What counts as realistic to one generation will seem implausibly 'unrealistic' to another. The melodramatic acting of the silent film era – parodied in *Singing in the Rain* (1952) – and the attempts to create naturalistic sets in 'gritty' realistic police dramas in the 1960s (*Z Cars*) are not perceived as real by today's audiences. And, of course, to audiences in the 1930s and 1940s, black and white film stock conveyed realism while colour was reserved for fantasy and historical adventure (*The Wizard of Oz*, 1939, and *The Adventures of Robin Hood*, 1938). For today's younger audiences, colour is effortlessly associated with realism. More recently, Edgar Reitz played with these variable conventions in his *Heimat* series (1984), blending black and white with colour in his depiction of the historical past. On some occasions, he clearly employed colour to highlight the emotional recollections of a particular character (using colour expressionistically), but on others he used colour and black and white apparently interchangeably, inviting audiences to question whether either chromatic code could lay more claim to realism than the other. This was another way of indicating the conventional nature of all visual realistic codes.

The melodrama of Bollywood – in films like the school-based, teen drama *Kuch Kuch Hota Hai* (1998) – is perceived as a form of realism in the same way that musicals like *Grease* (1978) or *Fame* (1980) were, suggesting that the codes of realism are as variable culturally as they are historically.

Realism: an ideological version of reality

We have established that realism, and TV dramas relying on realism, can therefore only provide a version of reality – points of view about the reality depicted. The points of view may reflect the writer's, director's, producer's or broadcaster's views, or (more likely) a combination of these, or it may reflect what they collectively believe the majority of their audience think. *Bodies*, for example, is not just a drama about life in a London teaching hospital; it raises serious issues about how funding and management affect patient care; *ER* tends to remind audiences that it is set in a publicly funded teaching hospital and is thus open to all patients. The version of reality conveyed, therefore, is always accompanied by points of view about what is being shown and thus provides a framework for shaping audience points of view: eg, in these medical drama examples emphasise the strains but fundamental importance of publicly funded health services.

In so doing, realism organises the real world into a hierarchy of values, attitudes and beliefs. It gives prominence to particular views over others. You might take *Teachers* (Channel 4, 2001–4) as a simple example. It focused primarily on teachers rather than students; it heightened and exaggerated for comic effect a number of elements about education (teacher briefing, management initiatives, inspections, pressures of marking); it generally highlighted sexuality; and it tended to foreground teachers rather than students, who only made brief appearances and were thus apparently marginal to the representation of schools. In this drama, the views and experiences of teachers dominated. And you could add that in order to appeal to audiences, producers created a kind of realism which stressed pace and sexiness needed to sell the drama to a broadcaster who wanted to attract the commercially lucrative 17–34 demographic. Audience and institutional factors, therefore, not only shaped the nature of the product, they also shaped the kind of realism it employed. In doing this, it established values based on sexuality, relationships, humour and fun. If you turn to *Casualty*, the emphasis is rather more on humanist values – on the need for mutual support, on the importance of an altruistic set of moral codes and a dedication to professional duties. In *Grey's Anatomy*, competitiveness is stressed, through the highly competitive world of internships within a health environment based on status and finance.

Worksheet 11: Different kinds of realism

To access student worksheets and other online materials go to *Teaching TV Drama* at **www.bfi.org.uk/tfms** and enter User name: **tvdrama@bfi.org.uk** and Password: **te0310dr**.

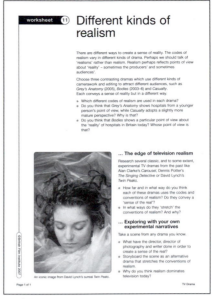

worksheet 11 Different kinds of realism

There are different ways to create a sense of reality. The codes of realism vary in different kinds of drama. Perhaps we should talk of 'realisms' rather than realism. Realism perhaps reflects points of view about 'reality' – sometimes the producers' and sometimes audiences'.

Choose three contrasting dramas which use different kinds of camerawork and editing to attract different audiences, such as *Grey's Anatomy* (2005), *Bodies* (2003–6) and *Casualty*. Each conveys a sense of reality but in a different way.

● Which different codes of realism are used in each drama?
● Do you think that *Grey's Anatomy* shows hospitals from a younger person's point of view, while *Casualty* adopts a slightly more mature perspective? Why is that?
● Do you think that *Bodies* shows a particular point of view about the 'reality' of hospitals in Britain today? Whose point of view is that?

... The edge of television realism

Research several classic, and to some extent, experimental dramas from the past like Alan Clarke's *Carousel*, Dennis Potter's *The Singing Detective* or David Lynch's *Twin Peaks*.

● How far and in what way do you think each of these dramas uses the codes and conventions of realism? Do they convey a 'sense of the real'?
● In what ways do they 'stretch' the conventions of realism? And why?

... Exploring with your own experimental narratives

Take a scene from any drama you know.

● What have the director, director of photography and writer done in order to create a sense of the real?
● Storyboard the scene as an alternative drama that stretches the conventions of realism.
● Why do you think realism dominates television today?

An iconic image from David Lynch's surreal *Twin Peaks*.

Page 1 of 1   TV Drama

1 of 2 pages

Realism – a relative term

Realism – or more accurately 'realisms' – is thus a relative term. Whatever form it takes, it has undeniably become dominant in TV drama. Indeed, alternatives to realism are uncommon. Some dramas stretch the conventions of realism while still using and exploiting its codes. For example, the stylised camerawork, silences and music emphasising psychological alienation in Alan Bleasdale's *The Boys from the Blackstuff* (BBC2, 1982) or the postmodern surrealism of *Twin Peaks* (1990) exploit and stretch realist conventions. *The Singing Detective* (BBC2, 1986), with its male-oriented, if not misogynistic, film noir narrative rooted in the psychological repressions of the psoriasis-ridden Philip Marlow and blended with significant childhood recollections and popular song, represents another form of stretched realism (recently mimicked by Peter Bowker in *Blackpool*). While the spare but grotesquely comic world of Alan Clarke, of which there are doubtless strains in Paul Abbott's *Shameless* (Company for Channel 4, 2004), demonstrates another kind of stylised realism.

The dominance of realism is perhaps not surprising for a medium which aims to reach a mass audience; but even channels which target minority audiences have not tended to experiment with non-realist forms. You have to turn to single dramas screened on television – ironically the origins of TV drama with the experimental broadcast of a Pirandello play in 1930 – before you get a sense of that. You might think of televised versions of Samuel Beckett's 'abstract' drama, or Steven Berkoff's version of Kafka's *Metamorphosis* (1987). In view of the general absence of any alternatives, realism tends to reproduce consensus representations of reality, either directly or indirectly, rather than individual or alternative ones.

● Representation

> … the more closely media texts are analysed, the more evident the variety of gender representation becomes, particularly once it is recognised that many texts are capable of activating more than one audience reading. Furthermore, in an increasingly pluralistic media … minority perspectives and lifestyles may be found, often providing alternative views that challenge the dominant ideologies and patterns of representation. (O'Sullivan et al.,2003, p94)

> Fictional entertainment texts have an extremely complex relationship to audiences' sense of the real. (Branston and Stafford, 2006, p133)

A representation is essentially an image plus a point of view: representations inescapably suggest points of view about what they portray. A key issue, however, centres on how some representations of people or issues become widespread and thus dominant, while others (often those which are challenging) struggle to attract an audience and thus become marginal. As Tim O'Sullivan, Phil Rayner and Brian Dutton point out in relation to gender representation, there are now more opportunities, within an increasingly pluralistic media, for minority perspectives and challenging representations to be created and accessed (eg, via the internet). Nevertheless, those perspectives tend to remain in the minority and marginalised and with little power to affect majority values, attitudes and beliefs. And it is doubtless the case, as Gill Branston and Roy Stafford point out, that fictional entertainments, such as TV drama, have a complex relationship with audiences' sense of the real and that the representations they incorporate can be consciously interpreted and unconsciously assimilated in different ways. Despite this uncertainty, the relationship between representations and audiences' responses lies at the centre of Media Studies, for audiences' points of view are influenced by their experiences of media representation.

All case studies in Section 3 explore further examples of different representations (notably, law and order, terrorism, ethnicity and sexual orientation). This section aims to demonstrate the ideas underlying representation by looking briefly at examples of the representation of people and issues: gender, using *Desperate Housewives*, and terrorism, using *Spooks*.

In exploring any kind of representation, you need to establish:
● What view of people or issues is conveyed to audiences (the representation – image and point of view)?
● How is that view conveyed?
● How far are audiences positioned to take up a preferred view (and how far might audiences adopt oppositional or negotiated interpretations)?
● How far do the representations establish a framework for people's values, attitudes and beliefs?
● How far do the representations, therefore, conform or challenge dominant representations and ideologies?

Desparate Housewives

Take *Desperate Housewives* (2004–). You might start with the humorous graphic images from the title sequence. They portray a rush through human history via icons of art, starting with 'Eve' catching the falling apple and concluding with the drama's four main female characters firmly holding the 'forbidden fruit'. The connotations of that final image obviously suggest a point of view: that women's sexuality is also their power. The burden of being constrained, if not oppressed, within marital relationships (Egyptian 'mummy' with kids; Arnolfini's wife clearing up the jettisoned banana skin; the male of 'American Gothic' succumbing to the temptation of a younger woman as his wife recedes into the background to be compressed into a sardine tin; advertising iconography of a 1950s housewife burdened by groceries) gives way to challenge: Lichtenstein's image of Brad's tearful girlfriend, who punches Brad with the fully assertive power of cartoon violence.

Each image conveys a point of view and sets the drama's comic tone of female challenge and defiance. The drama is female-skewed in a comparable way to soap opera. The focus is undeniably on the housewives, and the drama's narrative enigma (a narrative structure evident in several US long-form dramas, most obviously *24*, *Lost*, *Invasion* and *Prison Break*) becomes the means of exploring various kinds of restriction or repression which the women experience as a result of their marriages. And the focus of the representation of those housewives, which is reinforced by camerawork, lighting, editing and costume, is sexuality. The representation suggests that sexuality defines women's identity in a way that is not true for men – even though Mike and Gabrielle's younger lover are both seen as objects of female desire.

However, if the drama's perspective is predominantly female – the Herbal Essences sponsorship trail suggests that Channel 4 is targeting a female audience – then the sexualised representation of women is not simply one of an objectifying male gaze.

How are women then represented in this drama? Are women shown as being in control of their sexuality, aware of its power to manipulate others? (At one point, Bree tells her daughter that she is a woman and women use their sexuality as power.) In that case, as Marjorie Garber commented about Marlene Dietrich's persona, women are closer to sexual subjects than sexual objects. However, is that need to assert power through sexuality symptomatic of women's lack of access to other forms of power and status? In which case, the representation is one of limited power within a patriarchal society. Or does the representation continue to pander to the male gaze, even demonising women as manipulators – like the contemporary femmes fatales of film's neo noirs, who use their sexuality to commit crimes and get away with it (as in Stephen Frears's *The Grifters*, 1990, or John Dahl's *The Last Seduction*, 1994)? This is yet another vestige of patriarchy – a way of demonising women in response to the perceived threat that their superiority poses to men, undermining men's sexual dominance, social power and status.

If there is ambiguity in the nature of the representations, there are also questions about whether women and men view these sexualised representations of women in the same way. Do women see their representation in terms of sexuality as a source of power, where women are clearly in control of their sexuality, and do men simply see the representations as sexually provocative, objects of their male gaze? Alternatively, audiences may interpret the representations as playing with familiar gender portrayals, fully aware of the current debates and ambiguities surrounding gender representation. This suggests that at least some audiences watch the series from a postmodern viewpoint, seeing the representations as self-conscious, playful images (like *Mayo*, *Footballers' Wives*, *Bad Girls*, *Cutting It* or *Hotel Babylon*). All of this points to the different responses different audiences can have to the same representation. And it might also indicate that writers, producers and broadcasters knowingly exploit a highly contentious and ambiguous representation of sexuality for maximum ratings.

Worksheet 12: Contemporary representations of gender

To access student worksheets and other online materials go to *Teaching TV Drama* at **www.bfi.org.uk/tfms** and enter User name: **tvdrama@bfi.org.uk** and Password: **te0310dr**.

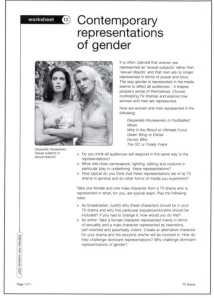

1 of 2 pages

Two points should emerge from any study of representation: that audiences are 'positioned' to adopt particular points of view towards representations (whether this is a preferred, negotiated or oppositional point of view); and that individual representations are selected from a range of possibilities. The key questions about representation, therefore, are just as much about how groups of people or issues are represented as why any particular representation has been selected.

Audience positioning

Stuart Hall developed the idea of audience positioning as a result of examining news reports on industrial strikes. In essence, he claimed that media representations established a framework for possible responses, like setting an agenda of issues to be raised with audiences, the responses to which would be likely to fall into three interpretative categories: dominant or preferred, oppositional and negotiated 'readings'.

Compare these three interpretations of the representation of terrorism from the opening sequence of *Spooks* (Series 3/Episode 10 – see case study in Section 3):

Dominant/preferred interpretation
- Audiences respond to the way the narrative is constructed and adopt the points of view implied;
- They identify with Fiona and Adam ('good' characters);
- They see the Iraqi surveillance team as a threat, even ruthless terrorists ('bad' characters);

- Britain and West – good;
- Iraq and Islamic terrorists – bad, a threat.

Oppositional
- Audiences reject the way the narrative is constructed and challenge the points of view implied;
- They do not identify with Fiona and Adam;
- They do not see the Iraqi man and woman as ruthless terrorists but empathise with their aims and see their action as a legitimate way of avenging US and British hostilities in Iraq;
- Britain and the West seen as bad;
- Iraq and Islamic terrorism seen as a necessary political challenge.

Negotiated
- Audiences partially accept the way the narrative is constructed but can see both points of view – the dominant/preferred and oppositional;
- They may identify in part with both Fiona and Adam and the Iraqi surveillance team.

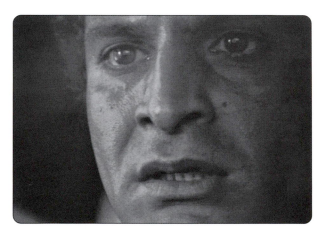

Characters and binary oppositions: How are audiences positioned to identify with Fiona and Adam and be antagonistic to Ahmed?

In simple terms, audiences who accept the most obvious interpretation of the representation, following the way the programme-makers have used editing, camerawork, costume and dialogue, take up a 'preferred' or 'dominant' position. 'Preferred' implies that this is how the programme-makers would like audiences to react; 'dominant', the alternative description, implies that the majority of people are likely to react in that way. 'Oppositional' suggests that the interpretation is in opposition to the preferred reading; and 'negotiated' implies that the interpretation emerges from a kind of negotiation between audiences and programme-makers.

Audiences might react in one of those three ways for a number of reasons: people's social and cultural background will play a significant role. An Iraqi, or someone with Islamic beliefs, might tend to adopt either an oppositional or a negotiated point of view. Similarly, anybody strongly opposed to the Iraq war is more likely to take up an oppositional or negotiated point of view. Possibly women may tend to react against the overtly ruthless position of the male terrorist and respond to the hints of slightly less ruthless views held by the female terrorist and thus take up a negotiated position. Within the current climate with Al Qaeda and Iraqi terrorism represented negatively in the news media, the majority of British audiences are likely to take up dominant/preferred positions. However, those who did not agree with the British and American invasion of Iraq but thought it justified may be uncertain and recognise the points of view voiced by Ahmed and Khatera. They are likely to adopt a negotiated position. Positioning is thus determined by the way the representations are incorporated in a narrative construction in conjunction with the social and cultural backgrounds of audiences – it is a product of the drama and audience responses.

Worksheet 13: Positioning audiences

To access student worksheets and other online materials go to *Teaching TV Drama* at **www.bfi.org.uk/tfms** and enter User name: **tvdrama@bfi.org.uk** and Password: **te0310dr**.

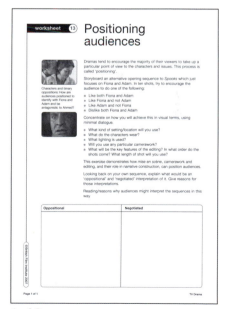

1 of 2 pages

● Ideology

What the study of genre, narrative and representation points to is the fact that everything in the media is not only a construction – providing representations of the world we live in rather than the real world – but an *ideological* construction. In other words, the images which comprise the media are images plus points of view about them – ideological representations. So what exactly does 'ideological' mean?

Put simply, an 'ideological' representation is one which is embedded with values, attitudes and beliefs about what is represented. Some writers describe these 'smaller-scale' ideologies as discourses, drawing attention to the structured language and images used to represent such issues. Barthes and Lévi-Strauss described these same features as myths, pointing to the constructed, representational nature of the ideologies – they have the status of myths rather than reality. What all three approaches emphasise is that what can appear as logical, rational, natural and based on common sense is in fact ideological, a constructed set of values, attitudes and beliefs which have grown up around people or issues as a result of media representations.

Section 3 includes some case studies which convey ideologies of criminal investigation, law, terrorism and gender. A good example is the representation of forensic science within criminal investigative drama (explored through *Life on Mars* and *CSI*). Audiences do not just see police at their work: they see representations of police using forensic science to catch criminals, which reassure audiences of the effectiveness of police investigative procedures and the criminal justice system generally. The view audiences receive of the police thus incorporates value judgements about them. I suggest that nobody can ever possess a value-free, 'objective' view of the police. There are simply different representations based on different sources of information and perceptions, all competing for our attention.

As a result of their interaction with the media, audiences gradually assimilate a cluster of representations of the police which affects how they see the police and view the criminal justice system. What people assimilate acts as a framework for their own views and for how they perceive. This is constantly open to change. Although it is a simplification, ideologies act like internal frameworks which shape how individuals come to think and feel, as much as how they articulate points of view, ideologies are ways of seeing.

A dominant ideology is the way the majority of people see issues. Any views which are alternative to that, or challenge it, tend to be 'marginalised'. Representations therefore tend either to reinforce or challenge dominant ideologies. In the *Spooks* episode, there is an attempt to explain why the two 'terrorists' act as they do, but the drama is weighted towards an official view of terrorism which suggests that it cannot be condoned. The sense of challenge is therefore weakened by the reinforcement of the dominant ideology of terrorism.

That example highlights another point. It is claimed that dominant ideologies derive from the values, attitudes and beliefs of those who have most power in society and tend to serve their interests. Antonio Gramsci voiced this view and used the term 'hegemony' (meaning dominance) to describe this. You might argue today that most power is held by the interests of business and government and that dominant ideologies serve these interests. Dominant ideologies, such as the importance of consumerism (fuelling lifestyle and self-image in, for example, *Desperate Housewives*), clearly serve the interests of business (and eventually of capitalism); the ideology that law and order is necessary for society to function and that the criminal justice system provides a safer society serves the interest of governments; and the ideology that governments can never give in to terrorism also serves government interests (as, for example, in *Spooks*). This is essentially the political force of the study of ideology.

The most accessible approach to ideology lies in investigating the degree to which dominant ideologies may be challenged by some TV dramas. And this itself appears subject to a power process. At any one time, according to Raymond Williams, there are:

- residual ideologies – ideologies which are still prevalent in the media but considered outdated;
- dominant ideologies – those dominant for contemporary society;
- emergent ideologies – those which challenge dominant ideologies.

Raymond Williams claimed that emergent ideologies – challenging ideologies – tended to be absorbed by dominant ideologies in ways which he considered retrogressive. Gender representation could be a (controversial) case in point. The stereotype of men being equated with action, power and violence, incapable of expressing any emotion or discussing feelings may be considered to be residual; arguably, the dominant ideology sees men as being capable of expressing emotion, prepared to discuss feelings but still prone to violent emotion and to exhibiting an acceptable degree of 'postmodern sexism'. An emergent ideology of the thoroughly 'new man', sensitive, open and able to express emotion naturally, prepared to swap power and position for paternal responsibilities, who treats women as equals rather than in terms of sexuality or can just as likely be openly gay, is arguably being absorbed into a more conservative dominant ideology closer to the stereotype of the residual dominant ideology. Section 3 attempts to explore the degree to which challenging representations achieve any media dominance, primarily through the representation of sexual orientation and social class in *Shameless* and *Six Feet Under*.

Thus, the key questions about ideology appear to be:

- What ideologies are conveyed by TV dramas?
- How far do these reinforce or challenge dominant ideologies?

- Why are these ideologies being conveyed?
- Whose interests are served by them (certain groups in society, whether powerful or not)?

● Institutions

What is an institution?

'Institution' is effectively a way of describing how large organisations work. By referring to broadcasting industries and the production companies which create programmes for them as institutions, we are talking about the way working practices and financial interests affect the nature of the products. Technically, therefore, studying the institutional relationship between production companies, distribution organisations (the primary role of broadcasters, although most also produce some of their own programmes) and a media product focuses on the impact of working practices, financial imperatives and regulatory frameworks on its products. It has always been the case that smaller, independent and alternative producers have to some degree challenged the dominance of the institutionalised aspect of the broadcasting industry. But at present, the rise of new media technologies – notably the internet and its potential – is widening what we understand by the 'institutional' nature of broadcasting. It will be interesting to see whether, or perhaps how, the internet gradually turns into an institution; certainly, media organisations are already attempting to institutionalise aspects of it. Nevertheless, it is possible for individuals to webcast, podcast and make public a range of media forms using the internet; and TV drama is already being distributed in this form.

Institutional issues

Studying the institutional aspects of TV drama raises the following issues:
- the significance of TV drama for broadcasters;
- the role of new media technologies and convergence in shaping future TV drama.

Despite the obvious importance of sport, drama is still one of television's most important genres and provides an anchor for terrestrial broadcasting schedules. Being a versatile genre, it is equally capable of guaranteeing quality (important to the BBC as part of its charter renewal, and ITV and Five in their attempt to compete in an increasingly difficult advertising market) as it is of reaching broad and indeed niche audiences (eg, ITV and Channel 4). It is television's 'film', and, indeed, several dramas have been released theatrically (eg, *Yasmin*) and frequently attract film-like production values: the co-production *Rome* (HBO/BBC, 2005), costing an unprecedented $100 million, to which the BBC contributed an undisclosed but again unprecedentedly high proportion, is only one conspicuous example. *Messiah*, *Bleak House*, *The West Wing* and *Six Feet Under* all in their different ways employ the high production values of film. The combination of prestige and popularity is seen in the way broadcasting institutions adapted and developed the genre to satisfy commercial imperatives, attract audiences and increasingly achieve high production values. This is noticeable in the rise of the drama series, which, from an audience point of view, combines pace, multiple storylines and the potential to explore characters over long periods, while also maintaining the advantages of narrative self-containment. The popularity of the TV drama crime series has been one major use of the series form. In this way, all broadcasters can sell products to overseas markets; commercial broadcasters can deliver audiences to advertisers and attract subscribers; while the BBC can maintain confidence in public service broadcasting.

TV drama has also been important to digital and satellite channels. UKTV Drama and UKTV Gold serve as outlets for the back catalogues of the BBC and the former Thames Television (now the independent Talkback Thames); BBC3 has provided a commissioning outlet for relatively low-budget dramas (eg, *Casanova* and *Funland*). As a means of attracting audiences to digital channels – an important platform in terrestrial broadcasters' attempts to broaden their programme share and compete with digital and satellite providers – an episode of a series is frequently shown first on terrestrial television, followed by the next episode broadcast immediately afterwards on a digital channel. Similarly, supplementary programming (such as 'behind the scenes' programmes like *Doctor Who Confidential*) are screened following terrestrial broadcasts of the dramas. More4 broadcast its comedy drama *A Very Social Secretary* on its launch night and has used the award-winning *West Wing*, a drama highly rated by adult audiences in Britain, to lure audiences to the digital channel.

**Worksheet 14: TV Drama –
Its role for broadcasters**

To access student worksheets and other online materials go to *Teaching TV Drama* at **www.bfi.org.uk/tfms** and enter User name: **tvdrama@bfi.org.uk** and Password: **te0310dr**.

1 of 2 pages

TV drama has also become a significant genre for HBO, the AOL Time Warner subsidiary, which started in 1972 as a small subscription channel but which has moved into film production and, importantly, high-quality but risky, challenging and alternative TV drama (*The Sopranos*, *Sex and the City*, *Six Feet Under, Rome*). It has benefited, in the US, from being a subscription channel, which has given it the editorial freedom to take risks in its explicit representations of sexuality (hetero- and homosexual), its raising of significant social issues (such as drugs) and in its use of language and a sophisticated approach to narrative structure. This has meant that viewers of such dramas in Britain have seen them broadcast on Channel 4 (*The Sopranos*, *Sex and the City* and *Six Feet Under*), which has a similar editorial commitment to alternative and challenging programming, deriving in part from the way it interprets its regulatory requirement to appeal to minority audiences.

The role of new media technologies and convergence

The web has already become a significant means of exhibiting and distributing media forms (advertising campaigns, animatics, mobile shorts as well as the variety of publishable forms such as blogs). Multiplatform distribution is obviously set to expand further – which, as the pace towards full convergence increases, will gradually turn broadcast drama into computer downloads.

Already, various forms of new media technologies are having an effect. Computer games have been exploited as a marketing device by the BBC – eg, the *Spooks* website ('Become a Spook') – and experiments with interactive dramas have been developed (*Casualty*), although so far only in terms of narrative outcomes being voted for. *Doctor Who* in particular is constructed almost like a computer game. *Spooks* was one of the first TV dramas to be streamed in a form suitable for mobile phone exhibition. And new forms of distribution – publishing short drama directly on the web, a kind of 'podcasting' in visual form, and mobisodes, short extracts of dramas suitable for mobile phone viewing – are all currently at the experimental stage.

The BBC website: A website, by providing information on current and future programming, clearly has an important promotional function. However, the BBC's main promotion of its programmes is carried out through its television trailers, which have now become widespread, such that other commercial channels have complained that it gives the Corporation an unfair advantage.

Effectively, the website seems to be a way of turning audiences into purchasers, not only prepared to pay the annual licence fee but also to buy DVDs, and use mobile phones to play interactive games or even subscribe to TV dramas. It is also highly revealing about the way fandom can be significantly cultivated by industries.

Broadcast TV drama to computer downloads: As digital convergence moves ever nearer, so do opportunities to download a TV drama from internet sites. The broadcasting industry – in particular independent producers – is currently establishing distribution rights for dramas, to ensure they maintain revenues. The availability of digitised versions of TV drama on the internet could give rise to kind of moving image 'podcasting' and effectively provide alternatives to traditional broadcasting.

Worksheet 15: Programme supply and digital rights

1 of 2 pages

To access student worksheets and other online materials go to *Teaching TV Drama* at **www.bfi.org.uk/tfms** and enter User name: **tvdrama@bfi.org.uk** and Password: **te0310dr**.

● Audiences

Audiences can be labelled in different ways: fans, TV addicts, enthusiasts, couch potatoes, students, viewers and consumers. These labels imply different degrees of response – although they are all, I would suggest, active. However, there is a tension between the industry's view of audiences (as paying consumers to be delivered to advertisers or as subscribers and licence-fee holders) and audiences' own view of themselves as deriving pleasure from their viewing. The previous section incorporated most of the industry's tendency to treat audiences as consumers and looked at audience responses. The case studies will explore audience response through specific examples.

The following is a summary of the key audience issues:
● Audiences respond to generic conventions and indirectly shape genre.
● Audiences have different ways of viewing (from couch potatoes to fans and interactive consumers, from, apparently, the most passive to the most active).

- Different audiences can respond in different ways to the same dramas depending on their social or cultural backgrounds.
- The way audiences watch television today is shifting gradually to multichannel viewing environments, DVDs and their extras, mobisodes, downloaded and on-demand programmes; effectively audiences are being segmented by a shift from broadcasting to narrowcasting.
- Audiences tend to be shaped as consumers, subscribers and licence-fee payers and delivered to advertisers, creating a tension between audience pleasure and industry commodification.

Case studies

Case study 1: Crime – Broadcasters, genre and the representation of law and order

> ... criminals break the law, the law breaks criminals (Rough Guide to Cult Movies, p119).

Life on Mars

Openers

Crime is the most popular type of TV drama outside soaps and accounts for around 50% of all weekly drama scheduling. It has been broadcast in just about all forms: two-parters (like the BBC's *Messiah* or ITV's *Donovan*), crime series (like *Life on Mars*, BBC) and crime serials (like the BBC's adventurous, Potter-influenced hybrid *Blackpool*). As a subgenre, it gives a crime context to the basic conventions of TV drama:

Characters

- Investigators and criminals.

Narratives

- Generally demonstrate how criminals break the law and the law breaks criminals.

Mise en scène

- Police investigation rooms;
- Medical laboratories where forensic pathologists examine bodies;
- Scene-of-crime officers dressed in white protective clothing;
- Interrogation rooms and techniques (particularly the recording and two-way observation mirrors);
- Expressionistic, chiaroscuro lighting (rooted in film noir).

Camerawork and editing

- Cross-cutting, frequently fast-paced editing and the use of atmospheric, non-diegetic music.

There has also been an infinite variety of 'spins' on the genre so that we have seen every type of investigator and criminal in just about every kind of setting. Investigating figures have included the conventionally non-conformist detective (*Frost*), accompanied by the contrasting partner (*Morse*, *Dalziel and Pascoe*, *The Inspector Linley Mysteries*, *Midsomer Murders*); forensic scientists (*Silent Witness, Donovan, CSI*), police teams (*Prime Suspect*, the majority of US shows); paranormal experts (*Sea of Souls*); the supernatural intermediary (*The Medium*); the cold-case units (*Waking the Dead*); police station ensembles (*The Bill*, *55 Degrees North*); investigators in the (nostalgic) past (*Foyle's War* and Agatha Christie dramas such as *Miss Marple* and *Poirot*) and female detectives in rural and suburban settings (*Rosemary and Thyme* and *Murder in Suburbia*). And so the list goes on. What they all have in common are narratives based on criminal investigation and an essentially conservative ideology. They all reassure us of the ability of the police to investigate and solve crimes, thus giving audiences confidence in the criminal justice system. I would like to look briefly at two aspects of crime drama: broadcasters' approach to a popular (sub)genre like crime and what that suggests about genre; and the representation of law and order incorporated within crime dramas.

Worksheet 16: TV crime drama: Broadcasters' approach to genre

worksheet 16 TV crime drama: Broadcasters' approach to genre

The popularity of crime drama on TV

Crime drama is probably the most popular drama subgenre on television outside soap opera. The following should give you a rapid overview its popularity.

Look at a listings magazine and count roughly how many TV dramas are shown in one week, and how many of these are crime dramas. Exclude soaps and sitcoms.

● During the week of 20–8 October 2005, 15 out of 27 TV dramas, excluding soaps, were crime dramas – around 55%. If one includes the five soaps, the percentage is just below 50%.

Look at the table of a September week's Top 10 drama, based on BARB (Broadcasters' Audience Research Board) figures and reprinted in *Broadcast*'s weekly look at ratings (Week ending: 25 September 2005, *Broadcast*, 14 October 2005).

Scruffy police detective Jack Frost in *A Touch of Frost*

Top 10 Drama

	Title	Day	Start	Viewers (millions)	Channel	Last week
1	A Touch of Frost	Sun	20.25	10.28	ITV1	–
2	The Bill	Thu	20.00	8.19	ITV1	8
3	Casualty	Sat	20.20	7.57	BBC1	2
4	Waking the Dead	Mon	21.00	7.56	BBC1	–
5	The Bill	Wed	20.00	7.50	ITV1	6
6	Holby City	Tue	20.00	6.93	BBC1	3
7	Spooks	Thu	21.00	6.50	BBC1	4
8	Taggart	Fri	21.00	6.35	ITV1	10
9	Afterlife	Sat	21.10	6.00	ITV1	–
10	Waking the Dead	Sun	21.00	5.96	BBC1	1

● What does this table tell you about the popularity of crime drama on television?
● Are there any similarities in the scheduling of these crime dramas? What role does scheduling play in the popularity of a TV crime drama?

Page 1 of 3   TV Drama

1 of 2 pages

To access student worksheets and other online materials go to *Teaching TV Drama* at **www.bfi.org.uk/tfms** and enter User name: **tvdrama@bfi.org.uk** and Password: **te0310dr**.

● Broadcasters and the crime genre

Broadcasters have recognised audiences' potentially limitless appetite for crime drama: of course, by commissioning, producing and broadcasting such a large amount of crime drama (satisfying their own economic imperatives), broadcasters effectively create that audience appetite. Broadcasters have therefore always aimed to provide ever-differing variations on the basic conventions of crime drama.

One way of revealing the industry's approach to genre is to ask why particular crime dramas are commissioned. Commissioning editors and producers are committed to popular genres as ways of attracting audiences. As Jeff Ford, Channel 4's Director of Acquisitions, put it:

> Police dramas like *Without a Trace* or *The Closer* will never be out. Everyone is always obsessed by murder and mystery. The shows get tired, but not the genres. (*Broadcast*, 14 October 2005)

But there is also the desire to provide a new 'twist' on the genre. Tom Toumazis, Buena Vista International Television's senior Vice-President, commented about *In Justice*, a drama his Touchstone Television commissioned:

> When you look at investigative shows, the focus is on getting people in prison, but *In Justice* is a unique twist on crime and drama. (*Broadcast*, 14 October 2005)

We can demonstrate this by looking at a range of recently produced crime dramas. *55 Degrees North* (Zenith North for the BBC) combined an arguably more feminised sense of narrative (akin to *The Bill*) with a north-east regional setting, police corruption and a central black character lead. *Murder in Suburbia* (Carlton Television for ITV1) combines feminised policing with a lighter touch of whimsy (and is set firmly in suburbia), appealing to both female and male audiences. *Life on Mars* (Kudos for BBC1), on the face of it a breathtakingly risky concept (taking John Simm as DI Sam Tyler back to a 1970s world of maverick, potentially corrupt police, while also allowing a glamourised look at the decade's fashion, music and values), displays its difference in both its premise and in its contrast of past and present police methods. *The Ghost Squad* (Company for Channel 4, 2005) is a variation on the internal affairs investigative model and is targeted at a young demographic through its youthful central leads and pacy camerawork and editing (it is loosely based on a former Metropolitan Police squad). *Murder Prevention* (Worldwide TV for Five) had a touch of *Minority Report*, with a futuristic unit supposedly identifying crime before it had been committed. And *Conviction* (BBC3, later transferring to BBC2) combined a rare challenging glimpse into police corruption, with fast-paced editing and much handheld camerawork.

● Representing law and order: Resolving crime drama narratives

For all this variety, the ideological diet presented to audiences is essentially, but not exclusively, conservative. Focusing on the way narratives are resolved in crime dramas is thus interesting. The main thrust of both Lévi-Strauss's and Todorov's claims about narrative structures is that they involve a reassuringly positive resolution in fiction not always attainable in reality. The majority of crime dramas do exactly that. However, some do raise questions at the same time, hinting that equilibrium is not entirely restored.

There is a range of resolutions, then. In *Messiah 4*, investigation eventually uncovers the female murderer (played by Helen McCrory). Her suicide reassuringly resolves the narrative, although she evades the full force of the criminal justice system. A *Dalziel and Pascoe* episode ('Heads You Lose, Tails You Win') shows how the murderer is eventually caught and dies, while ironically the private funding of hospitals, accompanied by corrupt entrepreneurial practice, succeeds. Episode 1 of *Life on Mars* teasingly captures a serial killer from the past, only to find that he has returned to murder 30 years later after his release from prison. And in the final episode of *55 Degrees North*, DI Nicky Cole (played by Don Gilet) – interestingly one of the few black protagonists in recent British crime dramas – captures the leaders of a criminal gang, during which a corrupt police officer is apparently shot. The final scene, however, revealed that the corrupt officer was being protected by the police.

In the same way, mainstream crime drama frequently, although not always, raises issues of gender and ethnic identity. For example, a now classic episode of *A Touch of Frost*, 'A Minority of One', plays with the perception that the police target black people as suspects. The narrative, in which Frost is partnered by a black officer (DC Tanner, played by Lennie James), shows Frost apparently equating criminality with blacks, being forced to realise that a white female informant only informs on blacks and eventually discovering that a black person is the culprit for a murder, which he had nevertheless committed under extreme emotional pressure. Frost recognises that the conviction of a black suspect will be in conflict with the public image of the police the Superintendent (Mullet/Bruce Alexander) is so concerned to safeguard.

The audience is clearly positioned to recognise the potential complexities of policing in a multi-ethnic environment and in fact the drama offers sympathetic representations of each black character, police and criminal alike. The training officer Tanner is shown as perceptive and not afraid to raise race issues; the young black suspect is eventually shown to be adolescent and merely on the fringe of petty criminality (while the main negative character is actually white); and the murderer is shown to have committed the crime under extenuating circumstances. It is a good example of mainstream crime drama attempting to set political agendas within the context of a positive image of the police and the integrity of criminal investigations.

It is relatively rare for TV crime dramas to challenge dominant ideologies about the police. Films as disturbing and challenging as, for example, John McNaughton's dispassionate *Henry: Portrait of a Serial Killer* (released in the UK, 1989) and David Fincher's *Seven* are not generally replicated in TV drama. The *Messiah* series, for example, mimics *Seven* with its emotive spectacles of horror and narratives patterned with religious significance (as well as its attempt to imitate some of *Seven*'s tonal grading and high production values). However, whereas *Seven* (1995) concludes with a disturbing challenge to the power of law to resolve violent crime, *Messiah* generally ends with the satisfying spectacle of the perpetrator being caught. *Conviction* and *Long Low Sun*, in their exposure of police conspiracy, are however recent, untypical examples of television crime dramas challenging dominant ideologies of the police.

● Representing law and order: police procedures in *Life on Mars* and *CSI*

Worksheet 17: Representation of the police

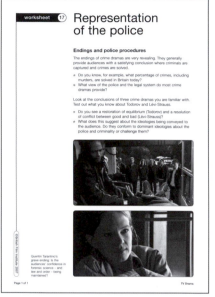

worksheet ⑰ Representation of the police

Endings and police procedures

The endings of crime dramas are very revealing. They generally provide audiences with a satisfying conclusion where criminals are captured and crimes are solved.

● Do you know, for example, what percentage of crimes, including murders, are solved in Britain today?
● What view of the police and the legal system do most crime dramas provide?

Look at the conclusions of three crime dramas you are familiar with. Test out what you know about Todorov and Lévi-Strauss.

● Do you see a restoration of equilibrium (Todorov) and a resolution of conflict between good and bad (Lévi-Strauss)?
● What does this suggest about the ideologies being conveyed to the audience. Do they conform to dominant ideologies about the police and criminality or challenge them?

Quentin Tarantino's grave ending: Is the audiences' confidence in forensic science – and law and order – being maintained?

Page 1 of 1   TV Drama

1 of 2 pages

To access student worksheets and other online materials go to *Teaching TV Drama* at **www.bfi.org.uk/tfms** and enter User name: **tvdrama@bfi.org.uk** and Password: **te0310dr**.

The premise of *Life on Mars*, characterised by John Simm as *Back to the Future* meets *The Sweeney*, dramatises the tension between police investigative procedures in the 1970s and the present. DI Sam Tyler (played by Simm) is constantly represented as shocked at the conjecture, gut instinct and lack of firm, scientific evidence used to secure a conviction. And in a basic way, audiences are positioned to find police methods of 1973 unsafe and open to corruption, which has the effect of offering reassurance that today's forensic methods lead to secure and just convictions. It is a clear binary opposition. However, the context for that representation is constantly questioned, so that the resolution of that main binary conflict is more ambiguous. Episode 2, for example, pitches the gut instinct of DCI Gene Hunt against what he describes, with neat period reconstruction of 1970s' unreconstructed attitudes, as 'gayboy science'. In the successful solution of the crime, established through a combination of forensic insight and rational reconstruction with a hint of gut instinct, the two officers clearly use elements of both methods. In terms of narrative, forensic science alone is shown to be insufficient to establish complete justice. A little of the Gene Hunt formula is still necessary; and indeed, he is not portrayed as corrupt so much as relying on experience and instinct in a maverick way. When you add the psychological context for the drama – that the narrative is based on a projection of Sam Tyler's attempt to save his life while in a coma – you sense that his own struggle to survive is also being expressed in terms of a tension between policing methods – between gut instinct and forensic evidence. In other words, Sam Tyler has doubts about current policing methods which rely on correct procedures and an absolute confidence in the empirical claims of forensic science – which might indeed reflect audiences' doubts that policing methods favour the criminal rather than the police.

The adviser on *Life on Mars*, Steve Crimmins, a police cadet in the 1970s and now a 'detective chief inspector with Greater Manchester Police', was featured in the *Radio Times* appealing to precisely that audience doubt. He comments on the 'then and now' of policing:

> The police were more effective back then … I'm not saying those tactics are right, but they were right for the age and they worked. The Police and Criminal Evidence Act of 1984 changed absolutely everything … . The new system is probably not as effective, but it has introduced great integrity into proceedings. And that's probably true of policing in general. (*Radio Times*, 7–13 January 2006, promotional feature on *Life on Mars*, also the cover image of that edition)

The representation of law and order foregrounds the integrity of current policing methods but does hint at the need to evaluate it.

The *CSI* franchise makes an interesting comparison. The series are predicated on the accuracy of forensic science and aim to reassure audiences of the integrity of the procedures. Season 2, Episode 1 of *CSI:NY* is a typical example of the series' representation of forensic investigation. Forensics take centre stage in the series: high key lighting, clinical lab equipment and computer imaging characterise the *mise en scène*, connoting sophisticated investigative procedures and clinical precision. The investigation team is constantly reaching breathtaking conclusions from the slightest details of evidence. Like *Life on Mars*'s shots of humour, the representation in *CSI* is not simply limited to reassuring images of the powers of empirical research, for many scenes are humorously presented, accompanied by fast-paced editing and pop music soundtracks (as you might expect from Jerry Bruckheimer Television). It suggests a knowing response – at least by some audiences – as they see a Tarantino-like postmodern representation of forensics, one which knows that it is merely an image. Nevertheless, audiences probably come away with a sense of the reliability of forensic investigative methods. Interestingly, the episode of *CSI: Crime Scene Investigation* which Tarantino himself directed contained a challenge to forensic methods: an avenging father lures the CSI team into a near-fatal investigation in order to prove that his daughter was wrongly convicted on the basis of forensic evidence.

Case study 2: Bleak House –
Broadcasters and the literary adaptation

Bleak House (BBC1, 2005, prod Nigel Stafford-Clark, dir Justin Chadwick and Susanna White, scr Andrew Davies)

Bleak House

● Overview: classic drama – the literary adaptation

Institution

- Since the late 1960s, the literary adaptation – or 'classic', 'costume' or 'period' drama – has been an important cultural commodity to sell abroad, promoting heritage, lavish production values and literary heritage, and an image of Britain and its past (as Nelson (1997) calls it: 'national flagship piece with an eye to overseas sales');
- 'Period drama', as the BBC currently tends to call the literary adaptation, has always been important in justifying the licence fee. Is this exploiting the connotations of 'quality' drama for its own purposes?
- Recent examples, such as *Rome* and *Bleak House*, have strayed from simple literary adaptations in order to attract new audiences and to convince the government that the BBC attracts a cross-section of licence-fee payers;
- Higher production costs (*Pride and Prejudice* cost approximately £6 million in the mid 1990s and *Bleak House* allegedly £8 million, while *Rome*'s budget is normally quoted as approximately £60 million/$100 million) are met by co-production arrangements and thus need to reach broad and different audiences;
- It has thus become increasingly important to make productions accessible to that wider audience, a goal achieved mainly by emphasising romance, relationships and sexuality (coded to varying degrees). *Bleak House* was innovative in looking for a different, formal way of making the genre accessible.

Genre

- The genre is therefore shaped by institutional and audience constraints. More recently, it has focused on English or contemporary (classic) literature rather than on the range of European classic literature which featured in adaptations from the 1970s (Sartre, Heinrich Mann, Tolstoy, Zola, for example);

- Historical locations and sets, meticulous reconstruction of the historical past and the recreation of contemporary dress (with highly visible production values);
- Well-defined characters, encouraging audience identification, sympathy or antipathy;
- Clearly defined narratives which generally reach positive, ideal resolutions;
- Generally involving a romance element to narrative;
- The name by which the genre is known has fluctuated, emphasising variously literary pedigree (the 'classic serial' of 1950s and 1960s), its contrast from the harsh realities of contemporary society and a safe haven from the present ('historical drama'), lavish seductive spectacle, with a hint of sexuality – 'bodice-rippers' (costume drama) – and appealing to audience perceptions of the past in terms of broad historical periods ('period dramas').

Narrative
- Conforms to a conventional narrative structure which resolves any contradictions;
- Tendency to combine romance and relationship with a coded sense of the historical;
- Stressing human values.

Representations
- Clearly defined differences in gender (*Tipping the Velvet* represents an interesting challenge);
- Tendency for racial issues not to feature (*Daniel Deronda* and anti-Semitism is a challenging exception; dramas based on slavery in 18th century);
- Positive, heritage elements of Britain generally brought to the fore.

Audiences
- Can be interpreted in different ways by different audiences – gender, race and different cultures and societies;
- The genre has arguably become more popular recently;
- Has given rise to fandom in some instances – *Pride and Prejudice*, most notably – although audience views are strongly mediated by the press and cultivated by broadcasters' websites.

Audiences have little difficulty in identifying the genre of 'classic literary adaptation'. At the moment, it appears that 'historical drama' is reserved for drama based on historical figures and events – Channel 4's *Elizabeth* (2005), ITV's *Henry* (2004), BBC1's *Charles* (2003) – and 'period drama' for classic literary adaptations, such as *Bleak House*.

At the time of writing, the genre seems to be undergoing a surge in popularity following the success of BBC1's *Bleak House* (scripted by Andrew Davies and produced by Deep Indigo productions, responsible for *Warriors*, 1999, a drama exposing the savagery of the conflict between Croatia and Bosnia, and the Anthony Trollope adaptations *The Way We Live Now*, 2001, and *He Knew He Was Right*, 2004). The success of the current phase of the genre arguably dates back to *Middlemarch* (BBC2, 1994) and *Pride and Prejudice* (BBC1, 1995), where a pattern of co-production was established (notably between the BBC and WGBH Boston, a US public service broadcaster similar to BBC2). This tended to emphasise costume, historical verisimilitude and thus a broadly 'heritage' image of Britain. Although ITV and Channel 4 have both produced some examples of the genre (ITV has currently commissioned Andrew Davies to adapt Jane Austen's *Sense and Sensibility*), classic dramas have always been closely identified with British terrestrial broadcasters' need to fulfil conspicuously their public service brief. Co-production provides a financially viable way of achieving that, with opportunities to share high production costs and benefit from added overseas sales.

● Reaching new audiences

> … Well-defined central characters set in solid, identifiable locations inviting from the audience credibility in their worlds as a basis for identification and sympathy with character. (Nelson, 1997, p126)

What was distinctive about *Bleak House* was the way it successfully captured new and younger audiences. It is therefore a good example of how broadcasters and producers approach a conventional genre in order to make it accessible to a contemporary audience. The production incorporated all the fundamental conventions of period drama (clearly defined characters and meticulously recreated *mise en scène*) which audiences expect and relish. But it also employed more unconventionally contemporary camerawork and editing, the accelerated narrative pace of series drama (Nelson's 'flexi-narrative'), soap-like presentation and scheduling and a broad range of well-known television actors from a variety of different genres.

- **Presentation and scheduling**: Twice-weekly, 30-minute episodes, complete with cliffhangers and a scheduling designed to inherit *EastEnders* viewers. The similarity with soap was a strong feature of its promotion (although the claim that Dickens's serialised novel was equivalent to a soap is probably exaggerated – see Robert Giddings, 'Soft Soaping Dickens', 2005).

- **Contemporary visual style**: Fast-paced editing, transitions punctuated by a series of tableaux with flashbulb-like sound effects, camera ramping, predominantly handheld camerawork, a preference for (whip) pans rather than the conventional shot-reverse shot filming of dialogue and expressionistic, chiaroscuro lighting as part of an evocatively designed *mise en scène*.

- **Popular television actors**: Some of the actors were associated with literary adaptations (Charles Dance, Ian Richardson and Timothy West) but most of the cast were not closely identified with the genre (Johnny Vegas, Warren Clarke, Pauline Collins, Tom Georgeson, Phil Davis, Anne Reid, Liza Tarbuck, Hugo Speer – and Gillian Anderson, despite starring in Terence Davies's *The House of Mirth* (1999), is obviously better known from *The X-Files*).

The BBC's aim to reach new audiences for literary adaptations was also apparent in such productions as the Russell T Davies scripted *Casanova* (BBC3, 2004, then BBC2), which was full of a burlesque staginess and a carnivalesque revelry in spectacle, and the contemporary adaptations of Chaucer (*Canterbury Tales*, 2004) and Shakespeare, set variously, for example, in a celebrity chef's kitchen and a hairdressing salon (BBC1, 2005). Michael Winterbottom's adaptation of Laurence Sterne's *A Cock and Bull Story* (2005) featuring Steve Coogan, with a cameo appearance from Gillian Anderson, together with his earlier adaptation, *Jude* (1994), and Roger Michell's *Persuasion* (1995) represent the film world's comparable attempts to reach new audiences through visual stylisation and reinterpretation.

An immediate sense of this combination of the conventional and the unconventional is evident in *Bleak House*'s title sequence. (A comparison with the title sequence of Andrew Davies's 1995 adaptation of *Pride and Prejudice* underlines the point).

Bleak House title sequence:
- The visual style gives the impression of a less conventional drama, using contemporary graphic design (merged and superimposed images) within a short title sequence.
- The accompanying music is a motivic sample rather than developed theme music and hints at suspense and mystery while still retaining the recognisability of soap opera theme music.
- Icons of the drama (the will, scales of justice, seal, the bundle of letters from Lady Dedlock to Nemo, gun, medal) are scrolled downwards as the credits scroll upwards, connoting potential interrelationships as characters from all levels of society become linked by the notorious court case at the centre of the drama. Again, a stylised set of graphics for a title sequence.

Equally, *Bleak House*'s *mise en scène* is conventionally symbolic in its counterpoint of light and dark but also unconventionally stylised. The gloom of the law court, the murkiness and chaos of Krook's house, the chiaroscuro lighting of the Dedlocks' mansion and the lightness of Bleak House itself (the home of the altruistic John Jarndyce) are all highly stylised in their presentation.

Worksheet 18: Literary adaptations: Reaching new audiences

1 of 2 pages

To access student worksheets and
other online materials go to
Teaching TV Drama at
www.bfi.org.uk/tfms and enter
User name: **tvdrama@bfi.org.uk** and
Password: **te0310dr**.

Narrative structure and social criticism

The narrative exhibits a similar structure to soap opera in its use of multiple narrative strands. The main strands follow Esther and her relationship with John Jarndyce and Allan Woodcourt; Lady Dedlock's 'awful' secret, which has made her all but moribund and which Tulkinghorn sets out to uncover; and Richard and Ada's relationship. All of these narrative elements relate to the court case of Jarndyce and Jarndyce, the vehicle for exposing the futile and self-perpetuating bureaucracy of the legal system. The whole drama acts as a commentary on Victorian society, with its rifts between social classes and its well-intentioned but ultimately ineffectual philanthropy towards the destitute, urban poor.

Most of these narrative strands are presented in binary terms. The drama's emotional spine (a term Andrew Davies frequently uses and which derives from Robert McKee's and Syd Field's scriptwriting ideas) is the polarisation between Lady Dedlock's secret (which audiences are pointed to quite rapidly) and Tulkinghorn's attempt to expose it. This fundamental conflict, which underpins the narrative, raises several power issues. Lady Dedlock demonstrates a social mobility and assumption of aristocratic surface, which brings with it a criticism of the aristocratic values held by Sir Leicester Dedlock; and Tulkinghorn's claim that his sole consideration is Sir Leicester Dedlock, his baronetcy, family lineage and social standing highlights how the law serves and thus maintains the power of that aristocracy. There is no doubt about the way audiences are positioned here: they identify with Lady Dedlock and are antagonistic to Tulkinghorn. Lady Dedlock is the woman who is forced to renounce her lover and illegitimate daughter and live an emotionally repressed life because of the dictates of a social class and status she does not believe in. Tulkinghorn is presented as exploitative and manipulative in an almost motiveless way.

Flowing from that central character opposition, rooted in social class, are the more overtly positive values associated with the altruistic Jarndyce (even though buoyed by inherited wealth), the selfless Esther and the equally altruistic medical practices of Woodcourt. Significantly, none of these characters rely on the legal system to sustain themselves. It is Tulkinghorn and Vholes who obviously demonstrate the predatorily exploitative legal system, encapsulated in the futile court case itself. But that self-perpetuating legal system, like all forms of power, is only maintained by individuals who recognise it – like Richard Carstone, who relies on material gain without any motivation to be self-sufficient, or Sir Leicester Dedlock, who uses the law to protect his material interests and who pays a human cost through the loss of his wife. For *Bleak House* is effectively about the way every aspect of society is interdependent on others and how the actions of the most lofty have an impact on the lowest in society. Society is portrayed as a community – which is, of course, the kind of ideology which both Dickensian melodrama and contemporary soap opera, which *Bleak House* was being presented as, convey.

Challenging issues are raised through the drama's conventional narrative which resonate with contemporary audiences. These include the pressures on women in society, a challenge to aristocratic power through the rising middle classes, a cumbersome legal system which compromises social justice and a polarisation between the materially more well-off and the disenfranchised poor. These can easily be explored in binary terms with their corresponding representational oppositions (gender, social class, law and living outside the framework of law). However, the potential social criticism embedded within the narrative is compromised by two elements: the seductive production values of the drama and its near-utopian narrative resolution; and its setting in the historical past, which can encourage a complacent, retrospective viewing from the secure position of today's improved social conditions. Possible connections with today's society, where huge gaps between rich and poor are still evident and where the legal system still arguably favours those who can afford to use it, are potentially suppressed.

The way the binary oppositions are resolved in the conclusion of *Bleak House* is revealing. The 'happy ending' is overtly idealised: all the major characters dance with one another in the sunny outdoors at Esther and Allan's wedding celebrations. The image has an almost surreal, Fellini-like fantasy element to it, which James Cameron also exploited at the end of *Titanic* (1997). In *Bleak House*, the fantasy image creates an ambiguity about how far this idealistic resolution can be sustained and hints that it is based on audiences' need for a happy ending. This draws attention to what Lévi-Strauss and Barthes have always stressed: that fictional, narrative resolutions cannot be achieved in reality. *Bleak House*'s final image is of a society whose members are mutually dependent rather than mutually exploitative. Whether that is any more than a utopian fantasy is debatable. The final image is just that: an image.

Worksheet 19: Representations in *Bleak House*

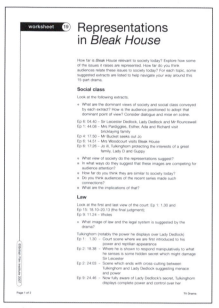

1 of 2 pages

To access student worksheets and other online materials go to *Teaching TV Drama* at **www.bfi.org.uk/tfms** and enter User name: **tvdrama@bfi.org.uk** and Password: **te0310dr**.

Bleak House

Case study 3: Spooks – Mainstream drama

Spooks (Kudos for BBC, 2002–)

Spooks

● Overview

Institution

- Kudos, an independent production company, producing drama for the BBC (reflecting the requirements of the 1990 Broadcasting Act, which stipulated that at least 25% of productions for public service broadcasters had to be produced independently)
- Mark Thompson, current Director-General of the BBC, has suggested that this percentage may increase (possibly to assure government that the BBC is not monopolising television production and thus increase likelihood of its public service charter renewal and continuation of licence-fee income);
- Marketing of drama emphasising the demands and glamour of an espionage world – 'MI5 not 9 to 5' (online applications to MI5 increased substantially after the series was first shown);
- Website – marketing, luring people into interactive involvement (pioneering game-playing);
- Mobile phone versions of drama – mobisodes;
- Role of the BBC interactive service – also part of the BBC's way of harnessing audiences.
- Scheduling – originally intended to provide an alternative to the Saturday-night film rental but later scheduled on a regular drama slot (Monday evening);

- Team of writers and directors, working within an overall series framework established by creator, producers and directors (comparisons with US style of series production).

Genre

- Positioned in between Bond and Le Carré, *Spooks* represents a modernising of the espionage drama genre – making it new and accessible to audiences, and using camerawork and editing techniques which attempt to appeal to a younger audience;
- Less fantasy, and a more 'realistic' image of MI5. A drama which emphasised ordinary people carrying out extraordinary roles (one of creator David Wolstoncroft's aims);
- Series has incorporated several topical security issues, and some controversial issues (Muslim extremists, suicide bombers – Al Qaeda terrorism).

Narrative

- Conventional structures;
- Characters conforming to type – functioning within binary oppositions/functional roles;
- A flexi-narrative rhythm, if not multiple narrative strands – binary rhythm of action and emotional reflection (appealing to male and female audiences);
- Raising issues through narrative but tending to reinforce dominant ideologies (using binary oppositional structures, restoration of equilibrium).

Representation

- Contemporary, easy to relate to but not generally challenging;
- Range of representations of characters, social issues, cultural and political issues;
- Create sense of debate.

Audiences

- Targeting/appeal;
- Differential readings;
- Involvement through interaction;
- Audiences as consumers and customers;
- Popularity – viewing figures.

Spooks is an interesting case study from the popular mainstream. It is neither 'cop nor doc' but sufficiently close to crime to make it attractive to mainstream audiences, for whom crime is the most popular TV drama subgenre. It attracted audiences of 8 million for its first episodes in most series, drew around 6 million for weekly episodes and 10 million for final, climactic episodes. Its approach to its subgenre is highly revealing: it represents a modern interpretation of the espionage drama genre, concentrating on what creator David Wolstoncroft thought of as a realistic image of an intelligence agency with ordinary characters performing extraordinary roles – hence separating it from Bond, Le Carré and indeed the more action-oriented and emotionally heightened *Alias*, *The Agency*, or *24*, with which it to some extent competed. And for a mainstream drama, it has raised some controversial contemporary issues (Islamic fundamentalism, Al Qaeda terrorism, the David Kelly affair), even if their resolution was ideologically conventional, as you would expect from a mainstream drama. It also attempted to reach a younger demographic through its pace and visual style, as well as attract female and male audiences through its narrative structure – a version of 'flexi-narrative' which consciously established a rhythm of intelligence-related action and emotional reflection (associated, even if stereotypically, with male and female audience interests).

It was produced by independent production company Kudos, subsequently responsible for *Hustle* (BBC1, 2004–), *Life on Mars* (BBC1, 2006) and *The Amazing Mrs Pritchard* (BBC1, 2006), and affords a means of exploring the relationship between independent producer and broadcaster. In addition, the BBC has used the drama to attract audiences to its digital and interactive services (episodes scheduled on terrestrial, with the following episode shown immediately afterwards on a digital channel, BBC3, as well as an interactive espionage game on its website). The BBC also commissioned an online games producer, Magic Lantern, to produce its first mobile phone video game, launched in November 2005. Indeed, it will be interesting to see to what extent complete TV dramas will be made available on mobile phones. All the central media issues can be explored through this kind of mainstream drama.

● Industry and audience: role of industry in shaping genre

The development of the series by Kudos reveals the role genre plays in industry decision-making and how genres come to combine expected conventions with variations on these.

Jim Sangster, in *Spooks Confidential*, the BBC's official handbook to accompany the series, describes the process from initial idea at Kudos to broadcasting on the BBC:

● **Producer – searching for something new**: '… Kudos producer, Stephen Garrett, was 'scouting for ideas to capitalise on the company's success with *Psychos* [a drama for Channel 4, also scripted by David Wolstoncroft]. Despairing of the trend in modern television to set everything in the same 'precinct' environment (mainly police stations and hospitals), Stephen set about trying to find a "precinct" that was untapped.' (Sangster, 2003, p22)

- **Developing the idea for the series – the producer spin on espionage**: He was prompted to consider a more modern approach to the world of espionage through John Le Carré. He was interested that espionage had not recently been the subject of a TV drama series (the most recent British TV series were the 1991 series *Sleepers*, *Cambridge Spies* (2003)) and approached David Wolstoncroft, to develop the idea for a series.

- **Commissioning producers – adding the hybrid element**: The series was originally developed with Channel 4 in mind but it was the BBC, through Gareth Neame, at that time the new Commissioning Editor, who commissioned the series. Neame suggested that: '… the series should become more of an intelligent action drama that could still deal with big spy issues' (Sangster, 2003, p23).

- **Scheduling and brief – broadcaster demands**: Initially the BBC considered scheduling the programme for Saturday night. Since audience research showed that Saturday-night audiences, if at home at all, were renting videos and DVDs rather than watching television, the programme was scheduled for a weekday slot – eventually it became Monday at 9.00 pm, which has subsequently become a drama scheduling slot which the BBC and ITV compete over. Lorraine Heggessey, then Controller of BBC1, asked for the drama to '… make television that would stop people renting videos' ibid, reiterated by Kudos producer, Jane Featherstone, on extras to the DVD of Series 1).

Worksheet 20: Industry and genre

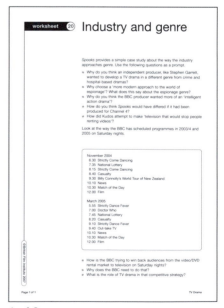

1 of 2 pages

To access student worksheets and other online materials go to *Teaching TV Drama* at **www.bfi.org.uk/tfms** and enter User name: **tvdrama@bfi.org.uk** and Password: **te0310dr**.

● Narrative structures and representational issues: binary oppositions

Focusing, for example, on Series 3, Episode 10, which deals with an Iraqi terrorist attempt to blow up the British Prime Minister and Arab diplomats at a meeting in London, the most obvious opposition is between the Western and Arab worlds – specifically, the British security services and Al Qaeda terrorists. The opposition is initially presented in terms of 'good' and 'evil'.

Value judgements are attached to each set of characters as they appear during the pre-title sequence. Audiences are clearly positioned to identify with Fiona and Adam, bathed in a light, mainly white *mise en scène*, and see those carrying out the surveillance, coded black inside a black vehicle, as a threat. The title sequence which follows emphasises that opposition: MI5 is presented as a protective power. As the episode progresses, audiences are presented with a range of polarities:

Good	Evil
Fiona and Adam	Khatera and Ahmed (who remain unnamed)
Western	Arab
British	Iraqi
British surveillance and intelligence	Al Qaeda surveillance and intelligence
'Ordinary' people's way of life (represented by Fiona, Adam and child – family)	Terrorist action which threatens ordinary people's way of life
Violence committed by MI5/ Fiona and Adam	Violence committed by terrorists
Decisions taken by British government: ruthless, lawful and necessary?	Decisions taken by Al Qaeda terrorists: ruthless, unlawful and gratuitous?
Government war – sanctioned action	Terrorism – unsanctioned action

Although that binary structure is quite apparent, interestingly the drama does question the US and British action in Iraq (innocent Western lives apparently more valued than innocent Iraqi lives), allowing audiences some licence to adopt negotiated or oppositional interpretations. This can of course lead to a contradiction: audiences may desire the successful release of Fiona and the killing of the Iraqi terrorist, Ahmed, while still adopting a position which sees the war in Iraq as wrong (those, for example, who protested against US and British action). The narrative resolution of these oppositions demonstrates their essentially conservative, ideological significance.

Worksheet 21: Narrative resolution

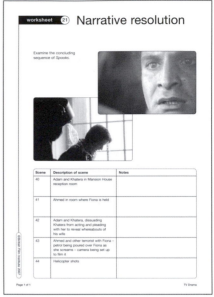

1 of 2 pages

● Representation

The most conspicuous representation issue in this episode is terrorism; but the way terrorism is portrayed raises questions about ethnic representation. For the Al Qaeda terrorists are Iraqi muslims; 'Butterfly', a plant, is Muslim; Zaf is British Asian; and Danny is black and British. The drama actually exposes ambiguous issues before concluding conventionally, thus reinforcing the dominant ideology that terrorism cannot be condoned and cannot replace a political process.

Audiences are nevertheless encouraged to debate some of the political issues underlying the terrorists' reasons for taking action:

● Scene 1 establishes clearly that terrorists are a threat: 'They have destroyed our world, we will destroy theirs';

● Scene 15 is intended to position audiences to see the ruthless tactics of Ahmed (through the cold-blooded shooting of 'Butterfly' as a double agent);

● Scene 19, with news footage in the background, portrays Ahmed giving voice to the view that Britain and the US have brought chaos and anarchy to Iraq. 'We are all Al Qaeda now.' Ahmed also asserts that the West is supposed to be civilised but 'you send laser-guided bombs to a wedding party';

● Scene 21: the lives of Arab children are worth far less than white …;

● Scene 24: Khatera – 'You never understand the anger you cause.' Adam – 'I guess we're all just puppets in the end';

- Scene 29: ruthlessness of British government representatives. The government cannot give in to terrorism;
- Scenes 31 and 32: shooting of Danny;
- Final scenes from 39 onwards: shows the extremism of terrorists – but also the human side through Khatera.

Danny's murder, the emotional centre of the drama – designed to create audience tension – is also the moment which represents terrorism at its most ruthless. Ahmed makes Adam choose between the execution of Danny or his wife, Fiona. He refuses to choose but Danny sacrifices himself before Adam is forced to make his decision. Danny makes ethnicity relevant when he reminds audiences of his background, and potential opposition to former colonialist Britain, when he states:

> You will never win. If I'd been born somewhere else, I might have been holding the gun. We don't get to choose those things. You're unlucky. You have lost your humanity. You have no kindness or pity left. Acts of hatred also produce acts of love. So you, my friend, will never win.

Both Danny and Adam appeal to human rather than political values – appropriate for a TV drama. In scene 31, for example, Adam pleads with Khatera that he is not 'talking about politics but talking about people' when he tries to persuade her not to go through with the demands of her terrorist partner.

Despite this conventional representation of the arguments surrounding terrorism, there is a hint that terrorists, intelligence officers and people in general (whether Iraqi, American or British) are all puppets to government agendas. Far from reinforcing a dominant ideology, this challenges it. But as with most mainstream dramas, more controversial issues are embedded within conventional narrative resolutions. The dramatic conclusion, in which Ahmed's attempt to set Fiona alight is foiled by the timely arrival of MI5 and Adam, remains the strongest image in audiences' minds.

Similarly, the conventional identification of Muslim with terrorist is only partially questioned, as it is subsumed in the final images of Ahmed's extreme action. (A previous episode, dealing with the suicide bombing committed by a Muslim boy radicalised by a cleric, led to complaints to Ofcom, which were not, however, upheld.) This questioning is achieved by exposing the reasons for Muslim terrorist action – to avenge US and UK action in Iraq set against the background of disenfranchised, impoverished people challenging US (and UK) economic dominance. But there is also a range of different Muslim characters to attempt to balance the representation: Zaf, Butterfly and Khatera are set against the more ruthless Ahmed. Indeed, Zaf jokes about an 'identity crisis' – 'British or Asian, it's tearing me apart' – which arguably sums up the contradictory experience of Muslim ethnic minorities in Britain today. Underlying this equation of Muslim and terrorist is the disturbingly prevalent mainstream media representation of Muslim people, from whatever national context, as a threat, if not potential terrorists.

Exploring the significance of representations in this drama thus involves evaluating how audiences' existing values, attitudes and beliefs act as frameworks for assimilating points of view. Comparisons of more stereotypical representations of Islamic people in *The Grid* with the arguably more challenging representations of British Asians in *Yasmin*, *Shameless* or *Bradford Riots* can be set against images of Islamic cultures in the mainstream news media. Some of the most challenging images of Islamic people – because they are of news footage of Iraqi, Afghan or Palestinian people – are to be found on the internet. These images do not appear to have the status of mainstream media images and do not therefore significantly challenge dominant representations.

Worksheet 22: Representation of terrorism and ethnicity in *Spooks*

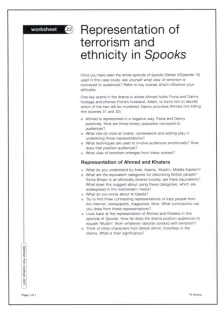

1 of 2 pages

To access student worksheets and other online materials go to *Teaching TV Drama* at **www.bfi.org.uk/tfms** and enter User name: **tvdrama@bfi.org.uk** and Password: **te0310dr**.

Case study 4: Doctor Who – Fantasy constructions and fans'-eye views

(BBC Wales for BBC, 2005–):

● Overview

Success and marketing

Doctor Who, at least in the eyes of its fans, can lay claim to being a phenomenon rather than a mere TV drama. Its first broadcast run from 1963 until 1989 made it, until recently, the longest-running drama (*Star Trek* has now toppled it). It has a vocal and committed fan base (its official fan magazine, *Doctor Who Monthly*, has been published since 1979, and its official website, www.gallifrey.com, attracts a considerable number of users). In keeping with former incarnations, *Doctor Who* reinvented itself once again in 2005, heralded by a TARDIS gatefold cover in the *Radio Times*, under the main auspices of self-confessed *Doctor Who* fan, Russell T Davies, writer of *Queer as Folk*. Mark Gatiss, actor from *The League of Gentlemen*, *Funland* and the recent BBC3 *Quatermass* (with David Tennant) and writer of 'The Unquiet Dead' and 'Coronation' episodes of *Doctor Who* (Series 1/Episode 3 and Series 2/Episode 7), acknowledged the role of the 'BBC publicity machine' in the drama's success (12th most popular television programme in 2005, with average viewing figures of 8.08 million, compared with 11.09 million of the most highly rated programme, *Coronation Street*). It was the subject of an unprecedented marketing campaign, which included a *Doctor Who* evening, major exposure in trailers, promotion in a broad range of publications and a whole sequence of *Radio Times* covers to maintain viewers' attention. It has since spawned rapidly released DVDs – some of which were released while the season was still being broadcast – as well as a plethora of publications, merchandising and a spin-off drama, *Torchwood*.

The drama was targeted at a Saturday-evening, family entertainment audience and was promoted by the BBC as a duo of programmes with *Strictly Come Dancing*. It also provided an opportunity to carry viewers over to BBC3 with additional behind-the-scenes programmes. The drama, originally developed by Sidney Newman in 1963 as an educational programme, where issues could be raised through the Doctor's time-travelling, has always been closely associated with the BBC's public service brief. In the run-up to the BBC's charter renewal, the programme's ability to draw in younger audiences, as well as committed fans and family viewers, will clearly support the BBC's case for continued financial support through the licence fee.

Fantasy constructions

One of the most fascinating aspects of *Doctor Who* is that its constructedness is conspicuous. All of its central features turn it into an example of 'postmodern' culture:

- Self-reflexiveness (drawing attention to its artificial, fantasy status);
- Frequent use of pastiche (as with the game-show parodies in the 'Bad Wolf' episodes);
- Special effects which draw attention to themselves (some of which are overtly artificial, even revelling in their 'tackiness');
- Constant fluctuation of tone via brisk, pithy dialogue (from frightening to humorous);
- Cult-like sense of costume (notably the Doctor's);
- Use of star guest appearances (eg, Zoe Wanamaker as the voice of Cassandra in 'The End of the World', Simon Callow in 'The Unquiet Dead', Penelope Wilton in 'Aliens of London', Richard Wilson in 'The Empty Child');
- The use of familiar television actors in cameo roles (Mark Benton, Annette Badland, Navin Chowdhry, Anna Maxwell Martin).

Some audiences – most obviously its fans – revel in the drama's artificial, overtly constructed, fantasy quality. According to Matt Hills (see reference below), some even talk in the same terms as media students, citing the drama as a 'postmodern pastiche'. In the spirit of postmodern self-reflexivity, episodes frequently incorporate references to and for fans. In 'Rose', the first episode of the 2005 series, a fan, humorously played by Mark Benton, is introduced to the audience. He has his own website based on the Doctor. In establishing for Rose that the Doctor only appears when people are in trouble, we are shown a 'fan pic' of the Doctor's ghostly presence at the assassination of John F Kennedy in 1963. This was the event which delayed the first episode of *Doctor Who* by 17 minutes and which has assumed almost iconic significance for the drama's fans – a moment when all certainties were lost and the possibility of a 'Doctor Who' was created (See Matt Hills, '*Doctor Who*', in Glen Creeber ed, *Fifty Key Television Programmes*, 2004).

In order to get some idea of how audiences respond to the drama, I carried out several small-scale focus-group interviews with some young adult viewers (17–30) and found that they were particularly enthusiastic about:

Mise en scène
- CGI effects (' The Unquiet Dead'/the metamorphosis of aliens in …);
- Alien creatures (some reassuringly tacky and fantastically improbable – 'Rose' episode);
- The TARDIS interior;
- Doctor Who's costume (as worn by David Tennant), which featured in much publicity prior to the 2006 series and in the February 2006 *Doctor Who* magazine as well as on the website;
- Mixture of real locations (iconic shots of London, shots of which show parts of Cardiff and environs) with studio sets – ' The End of the World'.

Characters

- Polarisation of heroic and evil;
- The Slithereens seemed to be the most popular alien, although most liked the reintroduction of the Daleks;
- The independence and adventurousness of Rose;
- Jokey, at times flirtatious, relationship between Doctor Who and his companion, Rose;
- Characters who take risks ('Rose', 'The Long Game', 'The Unquiet Dead');
- The cool of Doctor Who, who makes mistakes, which he jokes about, before going on to save the day.

Narratives

- Narratives which frighten and surprise you;
- Narratives which make you think ('The Unquiet Dead', 'Bad Wolf', 'Rose');
- Jokes and pastiche ('The Unquiet Dead' – Victorian Cardiff with Charles Dickens, 1940s Blitz episode, parodies of *Big Brother*, *The Weakest Link*, *Trinny and Susannah*;
- Bad Wolf Corporation – a touch of the Bond SPECTRE organisation here, and its media imperialism ideas;
- A similarity with computer games in some of the fantasy elements and in the way they invite audiences to become involved and make decisions (even if vicariously), looking at them as ways out of dilemmas as you attempt to get to the next level – layered narratives.

As you would expect, these young adult fans are not talking in media students' terms – of the impact of narrative construction, representation and a 'postmodern viewing position' – but their responses suggest how audiences subconsciously assimilate points of view. Let's look at three examples: the 'Doctor's new clothes'; the emphasis on Rose and other characters' preparedness to take control and challenge the status quo where necessary; and the significance of global media power suggested by the Bad Wolf Corporation.

Worksheet 23: *Doctor Who* and fans: Doing your own survey

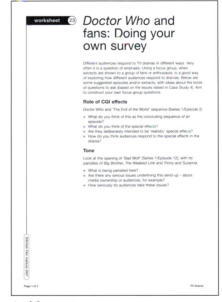

1 of 2 pages

● The Doctor's new clothes

In Issue 365 of the *Doctor Who Magazine* (Febuary 2006), there is a feature on the 'Doctor's New Clothes', where costume designer Louise Page explains the look of the tenth Doctor. Costume plays a highly significant part in the overall representation of characters in any drama, but it is particularly significant in *Doctor Who*. It is also an area highlighted by fans and the media alike.

There is an interesting overlap between fans' perceptions and representational issues: for in the very focus on the cult look, costume is underlining the distinctive, special powers of the Doctor. The overall connotation of the look is relaxed and cool, showing effortless authority and accessibility. The suit is not 'business formal' but cotton with a 'crumpled and messy', slightly retro feel to it; and it is in a softer brown rather than formal grey or navy blue. The long coat (a touch of *The Matrix*?) lends distinctiveness, authority and trendiness; and the plimsolls add 'coolness' to the whole image of authority. What then for fans are details of costume, which allow them to get closer to the drama and its actors/characters, is for the media student a confirmation that the image of power, positivity and popular saviour is being assimilated, even though not necessarily consciously articulated.

● 'Empowering' characters: Rose and Doctor Who

Fans also responded to the adventurousness and independence of Rose. In Episode 1 (2005), Rose is presented as an ordinary young woman, in an ordinary, not particularly fulfilling job, from an ordinary background (a single-parent family in a London council flat). Life offers no real excitements. When threatened by the mannequin, she attempts to challenge what she thinks must be a joke, but when she is cornered by them, the Doctor comes to her aid. Curious about this mysterious doctor, she is motivated to find out more and gradually becomes actively involved in responding to the threat. At the conclusion of the episode Rose is given the choice of returning to her mundane life or stepping out of it to go in search of 'adventure'. After initially hesitating, drawn by her (seemingly less mature) boyfriend, she opts for time travel. This could be interpreted in several ways, which you sense scriptwriters deliberately cater for. Her self-reliance and positive preparedness for experiences outside normal life lead to a kind of self-assurance she has not encountered before. And the knowledge she gains not only makes her more self-sufficient but also enables her to encourage others to take control (Gwyneth in 'The Unquiet Dead', Cathica in 'The Long Game'). However, her participation in the adventure, and the additional power she gains, could be seen as a metaphor for her transition to a mature sexuality. This motif is played with in several drama series catering primarily for teenage audiences – eg, *Buffy the Vampire Slayer* (1997–2003). Teen dramas seem to open up these potential narrative fantasies for younger viewers, who have reached a point in life when issues of maturity, individual self-assurance and power are particularly significant. That metaphorical interpretation is just about made explicit in the way sexuality is flirted with in the interaction between Rose and the Doctor (which was accentuated more in Series 2). There are several playful innuendos hinting at sexuality, sometimes in the form of the Doctor's apparent jealousy (of Jack and Adam in Series 1, for example). However, Rose is always shown to be in control. She is thus both perceived and portrayed as an independent young woman, in control of her sexuality but open and candid about her feelings. This representation is consistent with how women are portrayed in contemporary society and thus reinforces the dominant representations of them in the media today, which female fans in particular seem to have assimilated.

Worksheet 24: Representation of Rose

1 of 2 pages

To access student worksheets and other online materials go to *Teaching TV Drama* at **www.bfi.org.uk/tfms** and enter User name: **tvdrama@bfi.org.uk** and Password: **te0310dr**.

● Parody

Fans also appeared to respond knowingly to the jokes and parodies underlying the Bad Wolf Corporation. The game-show parodies of *The Weakest Link*, *Big Brother* and *Trinny and Susannah* comment sharply on the 'supposed' reality of game shows as well as raising other issues. Contestants in *Big Brother* clamber for what Andy Warhol described as '15 minutes of fame' and other lucrative deals (see 'Jade', *Guardian*, 25 May 2006). In *Doctor Who*, the Bad Wolf Corporation stages these reality game shows for 'real' – once eliminated, contestants die. Perhaps this hints that the *Big Brother* contestants' desire for celebrity status will kill them as individuals. But audiences are also parodied: it is our voracity for ever more extreme 'reality' television which demands the ultimate shock – a game played for contestants' survival. Luridly, that ultimate example of winning and losing keeps audiences watching. The theme of entertainment getting out of control is probably familiar to audiences – eg, *Jurassic Park* (1993), *Westworld*, (1973) or the more recent Japanese films *The Ring* (2002) and *Battle Royale* (2000). In keeping with the characteristic tone of *Doctor Who*, familiar issues are raised and reinforced through parody.

The Bad Wolf Corporation itself also plays with an idea familiar to audiences – the voracious power of global media owners like Rupert Murdoch or Bill Gates. Today's media conglomerates eat up their viewers and consumers. 'The Long Game' portrays an image of media imperialism which subjugates the human race. This aspect of the Bad Wolf Corporation is interesting: for in order to maintain absolute global media domination, the human race is both subjugated and held back to feed the 'media monster'.

The idea of totalitarian power and its corollary, human automatism, is after all a familiar trope from sci-fi (*Metropolis*, 1927, *1984*, 1984, *Brazil*, 1985, *Blade Runner*, 1982) and also appears in a similarly light, parodic context in James Bond films – most recently, in the parody of Rupert Murdoch and News Corporation in *Tomorrow Never Dies* (1997). It is another example of how audiences both recognise and are amused by this image of media power.

● Fandom as consumption

This links to the comparable tension between audiences and consumerism. Clearly, audiences see their viewing of TV dramas like *Doctor Who* as fundamentally a matter of pleasure; but from a media organisation's point of view, audiences are their source of profit and commercial viability. There is a sense in which fans, like all audiences, are created by media organisations. The BBC's website, with its interactive features, and the move towards television appearing on mobile phones (*Doctor Who* has created its 'tardisodes') are all part of that process, whereby 'content' is designed to secure audiences and, in the case of the BBC, a government charter and licence fees or, for commercial broadcasters, advertisers and profit for shareholders.

Case study 5: *Shameless* and *Six Feet Under* – The alternative and the challenging

Shameless (Company, now owned by All3Media, for Channel 4, 2004–) and
Six Feet Under (HBO, exec producers Greenblatt and Janollari, co-exec prod
Alan Poul and Christian Williams, prod and dir Alan Ball (and others),
created/written by Alan Ball, 2002–)

● Overview

Institution

HBO and the broadcasting environment of the American network:
- Alan Ball: working with HBO producers who actively encourage taking risks (branding image); introduce experimental elements to narrative;
- Title sequence and brand identification;
- *Six Feet Under*: a range of people involved in direction and writing; including Lisa Cholodenko, Miguel Arteta, Kathy Bates, Rose Troche, Michael Cuesta, Alan Taylor, Alan Poul. 'Studio' approach to production.

Channel 4: Company – All3Media:
- Like HBO, Channel 4 characteristically takes risks, due to its legislative commitment to cater to minority audiences, but also to capture a younger demographic;
- Other Company productions, its role within All3Media and its relationship with the broadcaster;
- Marketing images;
- Importance of alternative dramas to broadcasters;
- *Shameless*: Paul Abbott, creator and executive producer, overseeing a collaboratively produced series (like *Six Feet Under*'s 'studio' approach to production).

Text
- Title sequences and raising expectations.

Genre
- Alternative – extending;
- Characters (dysfunctional family) – identification.

Narrative
- Flexi-narrative;
- Binary oppositions;
- Journeys, narrative arcs (Chris Vogler).

Representation

- Family;
- Young people;
- Sexual orientation;
- Community.

Audiences

- Differential readings;
- Targeting of younger and alternative audiences?
- Fans.

● *Shameless* and *Six Feet Under*

Shameless and *Six Feet Under* display alternative and challenging features, both stylistically and in terms of their subject matter. *Shameless* uses a repertoire of overtly contemporary stylistic features such as handheld camerawork, jump-cuts and whip pans (to replace the more conventional shot-reverse shot continuity editing). These features still appear to be perceived as unconventional in the current televisual climate, even though they are obviously not new (with a recent heritage, in television terms, ranging from Steve Bochco's *NYPD Blue* (Channel 4, 1993–) and World Productions' *This Life* (BBC2, 1996–97), much youth-oriented drama and, of course, more recently *Bleak House*). *Six Feet Under*, on the other hand, uses high film production values and carefully controlled *mise en scène* alongside fantasy and surreal sequences to create an alternative visual style for the drama's challenging subject matter.

Shameless

Six Feet Under

Both dramas deal with challenging topics but in different ways. *Shameless*, variously described as 'The Simpsons on acid' (David Threlfall) or 'The Simpsons with the genitals graffitied in' (Mark Lawson), appears superficially to be the 'series that taste forgot' (James Rampton, *Independent*, 20 December 2005). Except that it is not that exactly. It takes risks in providing an at times grotesquely comic take on an unconventional family and the equally unconventional community they live in. The run-down council estate where they live – 'not exactly a Garden of Eden' according to Frank's voiceover – is named 'Chatsworth', a neat parody of city councils' tendency to borrow aristocratic names for roads and estates. And that irony further underlines its less than idyllic 'landscaping' (in contrast with the Derbyshire original). Its 'shameless' transgression of just about every moral code you could think of (a 'habit of flipping over moral assumptions like a joy-ridden motor', as Mark Lawson put it) becomes a kind of liberating anarchy – curiously close, I think, to the Ealing comedy world in which individuals subvert the bureaucratic and controlling structures of society.

For what is so striking about the comedy is the effortless way it positions audiences to identify with the Gallaghers. The plethora of explicit sex of most orientations, its easy accommodation of crime, drugs, benefit frauds and other scams are all subsumed within this anarchic, grotesque humour, which has at its centre an image of an 'unconditionally cohesive family' (Paul Abbott in the DVD interview) who support one another despite an absent mother and an all but absent father (who lives with Sheila but is mainly drunk or drugged when physically with his family). And just as the Gallaghers are a defiant family who accommodate each other's quirks, so the community they live in is a throwback to those mythic self-reliant communities of the past. *Shameless* is (as Paul Abbott has said) a title he hung onto for its 'irony': it implies others looking on and judging them as 'shameless'. The trick of the series is to cast the audience in the role of open tolerance towards all forms of shamelessness, whatever views they may hold outside the world of the series. As Paul Abbott has observed (DVD interview), despite its shamelessly explicit depiction of sex, the drama attracts a cross-section of viewers, who appear to respond to its underlying warmth.

Six Feet Under is arguably most challenging in its representation of gay sexuality. It places centre stage a gay character, and deals with his failed relationships and sexual identity (essentially an attempt to find an identity that is compatible with his conservative attitudes and religious convictions), as well as raising issues about the social acceptability of different sexual orientations. In addition, the drama emphasises the psychological in a way rarely seen in contemporary drama series, exploring potentially uncomfortable psychological features of all characters (most of whom are portrayed as psychologically 'wounded' or repressed). As part of that exploration, there is a slower-paced narrative together with several fantasy and surreal sequences, which serve as a psychological projection of characters' anxieties. Significantly, many of these fantasies centre on Nathaniel (senior), the dead father, suggesting that the need for psychological liberation stems from his former controlling, even patriarchal role (an authority that is parodied in *Shameless*?).

● HBO and Channel 4: alternative drama from alternative channels

It is of course significant that these more challenging dramas are broadcast and commissioned by channels associated with alternative programming. Channel 4 – which broadcasts both series in the UK – bought the screening rights to *Six Feet Under* from cable network producers HBO. Channel 4 is statutorily obliged to produce programming to cater for minority audiences following the terms of its charter. From 1982, the year of its establishment, to 1993, Channel 4 operated under a budget awarded by the ITV companies. However, since 1993, it has been responsible for securing its own advertising and thus there is a closer correlation between its programming and advertising. It has interpreted its mission to cater for minority audiences liberally since 1993 and has been successful in attracting the lucrative 17–34 demographic (*Big Brother* accounted for 18.8% of its audience share in 2006). However, it has continued its commitment to dramas which raise controversial issues. Channel 4 has actually managed to sustain advertisers through niche broadcasting, delivering niche audiences with definable profiles. Indeed, it still markets itself as a channel with controversial and original programming. *Shameless* was produced by Company (founded by former BBC Drama Commissioning Editor, George Faber, with Charles Pattinson), an independent production company, which has recently been taken over by larger independents All3Media.

HBO, a cable channel, producer and now a subsidiary of AOL Time Warner, was originally set up in 1972 as a monthly subscription channel, broadcasting 18 and R certificate films uncut. It moved into producing its own films and dramas in the late 1970s. As a cable channel, it is not subject to the same broadcasting restrictions as the public US channels and has thus developed a policy of controversial programming as part of its marketing image. More recently, it been responsible for some particularly innovative TV dramas like *Sex and the City*, the prison drama *Oz*, *The Sopranos* and, of course, *Rome*, co-produced with the BBC. Paul Condon, in *Six Feet Under: The Unofficial Guide* (2002, p10), puts it like this:

> One of the main reasons that *Six Feet Under* is able to break through the barriers of predictability and responsibility is because of the TV network that it's broadcast on. All of the main US networks (ABC, NBC, CBS, Fox, WB and UPN) are governed by very strict codes about what is acceptable and what is not. The level of bad language, sex, nudity and violence that can be shown on the main networks is therefore strictly controlled. Furthermore, as these networks carry advertising, they have to produce programmes within which companies are willing to purchase advertising time. Programmes that are controversial, which offend family values groups that claim to represent large segments of the TV audience, are very rarely given the green light to go into production.

Indeed, Alan Ball has famously commented that HBO producers actively encouraged him to introduce more challenging elements to the pilot episode (DVD commentary). Paul Abbott enjoyed a similar licence with Channel 4: 'I love the fact that nowhere else in the world could you put this sort of stuff on TV. I sit there thinking, "I can write exactly what I want"' (cited by James Rampton, *Independent*, 20 December 2005). Indeed, Paul Abbott is negotiating with BBC America to look into the possibility of broadcasting *Shameless* there or re-making it for US audiences.

The two dramas thus make a provocative comparison. Both feature unconventional families, superficially but not actually dysfunctional; both represent different sexual orientations positively; but whereas *Six Feet Under* characteristically focuses on repression, and characters' attempts to liberate themselves from it, *Shameless* revels in the lack of it.

● Creating expectations of the alternative: title sequences

Worksheet 25: Title sequences:
Shameless and *Six Feet Under*

1 of 2 pages

To access student worksheets and
other online materials go to
Teaching TV Drama at
www.bfi.org.uk/tfms and enter
User name: **tvdrama@bfi.org.uk** and
Password: **te0310dr**.

The title sequences of each drama signal and create expectations of their alternative status. *Shameless'* title sequence juxtaposes images of a council estate, a family and their home and community gathered round a fire with Frank's voiceover. The warming fire, of course, turns out to be a burning car. Frank's first-person voiceover – an innovative approach to a title sequence, capturing the tone of introductory voiceovers from past iconic series like *The Fugitive* (1964–7) or the current *Hustle* (BBC1, 2004–) and *Desperate Housewives* (Buena Vista Television/Channel 4, 2004) – anchors the images ironically. Frank declares that nobody says that the Chatsworth estate is a Garden of Eden (cue high-angle shot of a variously coloured geometric play area and some back gardens) and introduces us to his family through a set of ironic vignettes (eg, Lip's sex lesson as he attentively watches a demonstration of how to put on a condom; the simultaneous push-and-pull shot as Carl's shaved head approaches the camera; Debbie, the angel, shot with a fish-eye-lens effect before being revealed sporting a French stick and knife positioned as a V sign). The sequence climaxes with a verbal résumé of the images at the drama's emotional centre: the three things vital to any community – space (shot of waste ground), neighbourliness (shot of Veronica and Kevin) and, most importantly, knowing how to throw a party (shot of burning car, cans being hurled at it and provocative gestures to the police). Murray Gold's fast-paced, indie-sounding music establishes an upbeat tone with connotations of fun and humour.

Six Feet Under's title sequence, by contrast, makes no reference to any characters and is more highly stylised (Alan Ball wanted something 'cinematic – unlike TV'). There is a tendency towards close-ups – extreme close-ups coupled with stylised dissolves (for example, to the intense bleached lighting suggestive of death) – as well as speed ramping (showing the suggestive fading of the flowers, an image drawn from a classical American painting, Lilly M Spencer's 'We Both Shall Fade', 1869). The visual motifs all point towards death. The images start with the sky (the bright blue Magritte-like skies of *American Beauty*, 1999), the single tree on a hill (heaven and earth?) and the crow, harbinger of death, and then continue with an elliptical narrative. This sketches in images the passage from death (hands parting) through the body's preparation in the mortuary to its final resting place 'six feet under'. It hints at portraying life as a 'journey' which is preyed on by the potential onset of death, a motif which will be picked up in the drama itself. The appearance of Alan Ball's credit on a gravestone and the final dissolves into graphics, as the lines appear under the single tree nourished by the coffin beneath, also emphasise the whimsicality of the sequence and of the drama to follow.

However, it is the way the images are combined with the music which sets much of the tone. The music starts with unsettling chords (suggestive of death bells), which are carefully synchronised with the key images (the hands parting, the gurney wheel turning, the body being wheeled down the corridor), before moving on to the more whimsical pizzicato strings and detuned mandolins Tom Newman had previously used in *American Beauty*. The sequence is shot through with an other-worldly repeated cor anglais motif. The overall effect is whimsical and humorous, with a hint of foreboding.

● *Shameless*: the representation of gay sexuality (Series 1/Episode 1)

The representation of gay sexuality within the first episode of the first series of *Shameless* raises interesting questions: why Paul Abbott decided to include a gay character in the family and introduce him in the first episode; and how this representation is distinct from the majority of representations of gay sexuality on television today (indeed, it may be challenging them). It is also symptomatic of the approach the drama characteristically takes to controversial issues. For the representation is shot through with humour, at times grotesque, before character and audience are positioned to accept it. The 'narrative arc' moves from Lip's accidental discovery of his brother Ian's gay pornographic magazines through Lip's incredulous reaction to the idea of anal sex, ending up with laughter and acceptance. The storyline does take in an episode of free fellatio by Lip's girlfriend, designed to uncover whether Ian finds girls stimulating, and Lip's interruption of Ian and married shopkeeper Kash having sex (betrayed by each having hurriedly put odd trainers on). And there is also a confrontation where Ian has to defend himself assertively and the amused maturity he shows when gazing at the naked body of his sleeping neighbour, Kevin. Audiences, as much as Lip, are taken from shock and possible incomprehension to humorous acceptance. The dialogue is a significant part of that representation process. When Lip and Ian confront one another, Lip accuses Ian of being a rent boy. Ian fights back by saying he knows what he is doing and that he has done just fine out of the relationship (two United football shirts, for example). Lip's final, grotesque abuse (calculated by Abbott to be politically challenging) draws on tabloid parody: ' "Fake Muslim cheats on white fundamentalist wife with gutless gay boy" '. Tells you more about United fans than anything. Audience laughter deflates that issue; whereas it is the characters' laughter which finally heralds Lip's broadening of mind and audience assent. Struggling to find anal sex anything but unnatural, he says that the anus was designed for 'one way traffic'. 'It just is.' There's a pause. Then Ian starts laughing, mimicking Lip: 'It just is.' At which point, Lip laughs too and audiences are drawn into acceptance of the issue.

Worksheet 26: Representation of gay sexuality

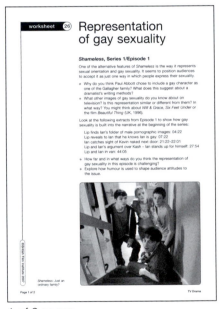

1 of 2 pages

To access student worksheets and other online materials go to *Teaching TV Drama* at **www.bfi.org.uk/tfms** and enter User name: **tvdrama@bfi.org.uk** and Password: **te0310dr**.

● *Six Feet Under* **and gay representation**

One of the most interesting aspects of *Six Feet Under*'s representation of gay sexuality is the presence of a repressed gay character, David, within a narrative that deals with a repressed family and their attempts to liberate themselves from repression. The focus of the representation is on the psychological dimensions of David's sexual orientation – his gradual recognition of his reasons for repressing it, the guilt he feels over its conflict with his religious convictions and his slow coming to terms publicly with it. In Series 1/Episode 2 (3:40–5:10), David wakes to kiss and embrace Keith (in what turns out to be the first occasion he has 'stayed over') before being interrupted by his father wondering which role David is to play and how 'this thing works'. This turns out to be a fantasy sequence and, as with all the fantasy sequences in *Six Feet Under*, it is a psychological projection of guilt and anxieties pointing to David's unease about his sexual orientation. But it also links with the idea that Nathaniel (senior's) death has the force of a release from patriarchal oppression. As Angela, the restorer brought in temporarily to replace Rico, puts it in a later episode (Series 1/Episode 10, 54:59–55:08): 'I've never known anybody be so uptight about being gay.'

An explicit exposure of homophobia (the opening scene of Episode 12), in which a gay person is brutally murdered following a homophobic attack, becomes the occasion for David's confrontation of his own sexual orientation. As David confesses to Keith, he loathes himself for the same religious reasons which fuel the protests of the Christian anti-homosexual fundamentalists at the funeral of the murdered gay Mark Foster (Series 1/Episode 12, 46:20–49:37). He attacks them for their prejudiced fundamentalism but cannot rid himself of those same attitudes. This is why the sequence where he reads in church from the Psalms is so significant: 'In thee O Lord, Let me put my trust. Let me never be ashamed.' Fantasy and the 'reality' of the drama blend together here. David suddenly imagines himself giving a sermon on the hypocrisy of spreading God's love throughout the world when he denies it to himself (drawing approval and applause from the congregation), only for this fantasy to collapse into the 'reality' of his psalm reading about not being ashamed. As is evident to his former boyfriend Keith, who is in the congregation, David's reading is a coded acceptance of his own sexual orientation and exposure of the restrictive attitudes of the Church. His mother, of course, misses both church and her son's reading, as she ends up having sex with Nikolai instead. And if that were not sufficient comment on the constraining, oppressive structures of religion, David is caught glancing at a stained-glass window, where a priest appears to be blessing an altar boy kneeling before him – a deeply and humorously ambiguous image.

● *Shameless*: using narrative structure to challenge

Shameless characteristically employs a multiple-narrative structure. The series tends not to use the flexi-narrative with quite the coherence of US series like *The Sopranos*, *ER* or *The West Wing*, for example, where the whole episode revolves around a single idea (frequently reflected in the title). However, it does use this narrative structure in a cumulative way to raise issues and challenge, juxtaposing apparently disparate ideas while moving from one bravura moral subversion to another. Series 3/Episode 4, contains a particularly good example of this. The central idea of the episode revolves around 'shopping a scrounger': it is a merciless exposure of Department of Social Security tactics to uncover benefits fraud. In what at times seems like the ethos of *Passport to Pimlico*, the Chatsworth estate is brought together to challenge government bureaucracy. The sequence of betrayals begins with Carol being 'shopped' for shoplifting on her grandson Marty's first day as the supermarket security guard. This collapses into Carol's vengeful 'shopping' of her friend who, she had recently found out, had slept with her husband at her wedding. This ushers in one of Frank's drunken, signature tirades against the DSS 'shop a scrounger campaign' and which draws together Orwell's Big Brother, socialism, (Lenin's) 'thin end of the wedge', Hitler, Bin Laden and Agincourt. This speech initiates the DSS fraud squad's parodic descent onto the estate. The action brings the community together in support of one another's scams: Lip gives advice at a fee; Carl and Frank double as characters who are being fraudulently claimed for. It is a series of farce-like caricatures, with camerawork reminiscent of Spud's interview in *Trainspotting* (1996) and gentle parodies of Frank Perry's 1968 *The Swimmer* (also used as the basis for a Levi advert), as Debbie and Carl step over gardens in mock exposure of the superficial social status and sham wealth they point to.

The whole narrative sequence of betrayals is framed by a fantasy: Sheila's fairy-tale-like fantasy, based on 'The Little Mermaid', that she will be proposed to. Her fantasy is in turn interwoven with Carl's fantasies about Lip's girlfriend, Emily, which leads him to 'shop' his brother. The two linked narrative strands merge when, in grotesque parody of the Last Supper (a 90-degree shot of a candlelit dinner table with Frank doubling as Christ), Frank is forced to betray himself by making good his proposal to Sheila in the pub's toilets. Frank's wildly inappropriate but somehow apt description of his relationship with Sheila ('love that dare not speak its name') is thus legitimised by the ring Sheila is allowed to purchase from a shopping channel. This blend of betrayal and fantasy concludes with victory for the estate against the DSS. Individual freedom and the powers of the community thus successfully defeat bureaucracy, suggesting that all attempt at control is fantasy, even the control underpinning relationships. As Sheila dances in a fantasy of bliss, feeling like a queen, audiences are treated to another of Frank's perceptions. He claims that a man has a very special feeling for the mother of his children (thinking of his first wife and addressing Lip, who is watching his girlfriend, Mandy, and his child): 'it's in your bones, just like when a cancer spreads and they give up on your chemo ...'.

Worksheet 27: Challenging alternatives?

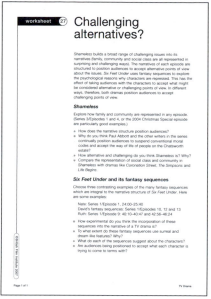

1 of 2 pages

To access student worksheets and other online materials go to *Teaching TV Drama* at **www.bfi.org.uk/tfms** and enter User name: **tvdrama@bfi.org.uk** and Password: **te0310dr**.

● *Six Feet Under*: using narrative structure for psychological projection

One of the most distinctive, if not radically alternative, features of the narrative structure of *Six Feet Under* is its use of fantasy sequences as psychological projections of characters' anxieties. Although the technique is familiar to audiences, it is an indication of the fundamentally psychological nature of this drama, which is not common. One of the primary exponents of this way of exploring psychology through surreal and fantasy sequences is of course Dennis Potter. His 1970s' drama *Double Dare* (BBC, 1976) is an early example of this. But it is *The Singing Detective* (BBC, 1986) where psychological projections and musical numbers are blended most creatively in three narrative strands, all of them rooted in the guilt and anxieties of the main character, Philip Marlow.

Nate's fear of death is first introduced as an anxiety going back to childhood experiences. It is later partially unravelled by Brenda (Series 1/Episode 9) when Nate reveals why he was so disturbed by Brenda's therapeutic role-plays (42:06–42:56). In the pilot episode (24:00), Nate ventures into his father's restoration room and is confronted with his father and a dead body. The sequence is portrayed with all the conventions of psychological horror. It starts with a handheld subjective camera revealing bare stone walls as a character descends a flight of stairs to a basement. The sequence is characterised by desaturated colour and the accompanying music is eerily foreboding. This mobile subjective shot is intercut with extreme close-ups of first garish, blue rubber gloves, then a scalpel, then blood being sucked down rubber tubing and finally, after a further scalpel shot, a close-up of the embalming fluid being pumped through tubing (alluding grotesquely to the advert for embalming fluid previously shown and its catchphrase 'only real life is better'). The subjective camera tracks through the glass door marked private to reveal, via a reverse shot, a young boy. The young boy watches his father smoking as he prepares a body laid out on the table. The music immediately cross-fades from suspenseful tones to Peggy Lee's 'I Love Being Here with You', while his father rests his cigarette and ashtray on the corpse's chest. His father reassures him that there is nothing to be afraid of but at the end of the sequence he leans menacingly forward towards the camera while thrusting a blue rubber glove in Nate's face, saying that he can touch the body if he wants. The Peggy Lee music becomes ambiguous: is it ironic (he hates being there with his father) or is it the expression of Nate's desire to be with his father? This raises the question of whether his fear of death relates to such childhood memories or whether it is a fear of losing someone he is prepared to commit to.

The fantasy images David experiences relate to anxieties and desires over his sexuality: in Episode 10 he humorously images himself being stabbed, only to be heroically saved by Keith; while his anxieties about not being ashamed of his gay sexuality are expressed through the persistent appearance in Episode 13 of the deformed body of Mark Foster, the murdered victim of the homophobic attack shown in the previous episode. The wish-fulfilment fantasy, which sees the congregation applauding his sermon-like sentiments in Episode 13 (mentioned above), acts as a psychological confirmation and encouragement to challenge the hypocritical religious roots of his shame.

Ruth experiences a similarly liberating fantasy sequence in Episode 9. This is amusingly induced by the ecstasy tablets she takes, thinking they are headache pills. Traditionally Freudian images – entering woods, dressed as a lost girl, hugging tree trunks, being confronted by a bear with an alarm clock – lead Ruth to a meeting with her husband, who gives his assent to her recapturing the sexual emotions they had lost after a life together. The sequence, a clear psychological projection of repressed emotions, fulfils the function of freeing Ruth from her repressed sexuality, to which Hiram jokingly alludes when declaring that she had never been this passionate with him.

Glossary

Audiences
Audiences can be labelled in different ways: fans, TV addicts, enthusiasts, couch potatoes, students, viewers and consumers. The labels imply different degrees of response. There is a tension between the industry's view of audiences (as paying consumers to be delivered to advertisers or as subscribers and licence-fee holders) and audiences' own view of themselves as deriving pleasure from their viewing.

Binary opposition
Lévi-Strauss, who first applied this principle to myths, claimed that narratives are constructed in terms of a conflict between opposites (characters, cultures, ideas) which audiences want to see resolved. He argued that resolutions are achieved in fiction but not in real life.

Conventions
The standard ingredients of a genre. The conventions at the root of all TV drama are characters, narratives and *mise en scène*.

Diegetic (and non-diegetic) sound
Diegetic sound is sound which is part of the scene itself; sound which is added later (in post-production), like sound effects and music, is non-diegetic.

Flexi-narrative
A term coined by Nelson in *Drama in Transition* (1995), it describes a narrative composed of different strands – a multiple narrative – and is most familiar to audiences from soap operas. Nelson claimed that drama series frequently used this technique in order to maintain audience interest.

Genre
A type of media text, like TV drama, game shows or documentaries, and a means of categorising different kinds of media. Genres balance industry and audience needs. They are subject to change, as broadcasters and audiences attempt to combine the familiar with the (slightly) unexpected. They tend to be conservative but can also raise questions in an accessible way.

Hegemony

Derived from the Greek word for 'leadership', hegemony refers to the supremacy of a dominant ideology. More specifically, it refers to the way dominant ideologies tend to serve the interests of the major power groups in a society. In today's terms, that probably means multinational business interests, including media conglomerates, and governments. In this context, it was first used by Antonio Gramsci (1971) in his *Prison Notebooks*.

Ideology

Literally, a set of values, attitudes and beliefs, it more accurately describes the values, attitudes and beliefs which people assimilate and which provide a framework for a way of seeing. Ideologies underlie all media like TV dramas and are assimilated by audiences to shape their own ideological outlooks.

Institutions

A way of describing the broadcasting industries and the production companies which create programmes for them. A study of institutions involves examining how their working practices, financial interests and regulatory frameworks affect the nature of the products.

Intertextuality

How media texts, like TV drama, gain additional significance by referring or alluding to other media texts.

Long-form drama

The range of dramas which unfold over several serialised episodes – serials, drama series, portmanteau dramas and continuing dramas (soap operas).

Mise en scène

'*Scène*' is the French word for 'stage': so this term literally means 'put on stage'. The term was borrowed from the theatre world and applied to cinema in the 1920s to refer to everything on stage for filming. Hence, *mise en scène* is what the camera films: eg, location, sets, props, lighting, costume and make-up.

Narrative

At their simplest, media narratives, whether in the form of TV drama, film or documentaries, are stories told in images. How the images are selected and pieced together determines the nature of the narrative.

Narrowcasting

Programmes which only reach minority, specialised (niche) audiences – ie, a narrow rather than a broad range of people. With more and varied platforms for viewing, 'broadcasting' to mass audiences might be replaced by 'narrowcasting' to audiences who watch programmes when they want on different platforms. This opens up the possibility of targeting highly specific audiences.

Positioning

Originally coined by Stuart Hall, it describes the processes by which audiences are encouraged to take up a particular point of view – a particular 'position'. Audiences are characteristically positioned by programme-makers to adopt a preferred interpretation of a representation. However, they may reject this and take an 'oppositional' view or only partially accept it (a 'negotiated' interpretation).

Postmodern

Examples of the media which play with genre and frequently make references to other media. They adopt a self-consciously artificial tone rather than attempt realism. Dramas like the recent *Mayo*, *Hotel Babylon* or *Footballers' Wives* all display aspects of the postmodern. *Twin Peaks* (1990) and Tarantino's 1994 film, *Pulp Fiction*, are classic examples.

Realism

A means of conveying a sense of the real using codes and conventions. Realism provides a version of reality rather than reality itself – an ideological representation of the real.

Representation

At its simplest, it is an image plus a point of view. A representation is the result of a process by which aspects of the real world are reconstructed in media texts and which necessarily involve points of view about what is depicted. The representations of groups of people, social issues and events, which make up media texts, are thus ideological. Another way of thinking about representation is to see the media as providing a framework in which different kinds of ideological representations compete for audience attention and thus dominance in society.

Simulacra

A term coined by Jean Baudrillard, who used the word 'simulacra' to indicate that all media representations were copies of previous media representations, which were themselves copies of earlier media representations. Media like TV dramas convey their sense of realism by referring to other TV dramas rather than to reality itself. As Baudrillard claims, it is almost that what people assume to be 'reality' is in fact a kind of 'hyperreality' – the artificial or heightened reality presented by the media. Media representations, including those of TV drama, dominate people's thinking so much that the world of the media becomes more real than the 'real' world.

References and resources

Books and articles

● TV drama: Book length studies

George Brandt (ed) 1993, *British TV Drama in the 1980s*, Cambridge University Press

Sarah Cardwell (2004), *Andrew Davies*, Manchester University Press

Lez Cooke (2003), *British Television Drama*, BFI

Glen Creeber (ed) (2001), *The Television Genre Book*, BFI

Glen Creeber (2004), *Serial Television: Big Drama on the Small Screen*, BFI

Glen Creeber (ed) (2004), *Fifty Key Television Programmes*, Arnold

Sean Day-Lewis (1998), *Talk of Drama: Views of the Television Dramatist Now and Then*, University of Luton Press

Jason Jacobs (2000), *The Intimate Screen: Early British Television Drama*, Oxford University Press

Robin Nelson (1997), *TV Drama in Transition: Forms, Values and Cultural Exchange*, Macmillan

Janine Pourroy (1996), *Behind the Scenes at ER*, Ebury Press

Jim Sangster (2003), *Spooks Confidential: The Official Guide*, Contender Books

Paul Simpson (ed) (2002), *The Rough Guide to Cult TV*, Rough Guides/distributed by Penguin

Sue Thornham and Tony Purvis (2005), *Television Drama: Theories and Identities*, Palgrave Macmillan

John Tulloch (1990), *Television Drama: Agency, Audience and Myth*, Routledge

● Television and Television Studies

Jonathan Bignall (2004), *Television Studies: An Introduction*, Routledge
   (includes an interesting section on gender representations and *Sex and the City*)
Graeme Burton (2000), *Talking TV*, Arnold
Bernadette Casey et al. (2000), *Television Studies: Key Concepts*, Routledge
Douglas Gomery (2000), *Who Owns the Media?*, Lawrence Erlbaum
David Lusted and Christine Geraghty (1990), *Television Studies Book*,
   Routledge
Alistair D McGown (2005), *BFI Television Handbook* 2005, BFI
Horace Newcomb (ed) (2002), *Television: The Critical View*, 6th edition,
   Oxford
Keith Selby and Ron Cowdery (1995), *How to Study Television*, Palgrave
   Macmillan
John Sinclair (ed) (2004), *Contemporary World Television*, BFI
Jeanette Steemers (2004), *Selling Television: British Television in the Global
   Marketplace*, BFI

● Genre, narrative and representation

Rick Altman (1999), *Film/Genre*, BFI
John Downing and Charles Husband (2005), *Representing Race*, Sage
Jane Feuer (1992), 'Genre Study and Television' in Robert C Allen (ed),
   *Channels of Discourse Reassembled: Television and Contemporary
   Criticism*, Routledge
Marjorie Garber (1992), 'Strike a Pose' (on Marlene Dietrich), *Sight and
   Sound*, September
Antonio Gramsci (1971), *Selections from the Prison Notebooks*, Lawrence
   and Wishart
Stuart Hall (ed) (1997), *Representation: Cultural Representations and
   Signifying Practices*, Sage in association with Open University
Wendy Helsby et al. (2005), *Studying Representation*, BFI
Nick Lacey (1998), *Image and Representation: Key Concepts in Media
   Studies*, Macmillan
Nick Lacey (2000), *Narrative and Genre*, Macmillan
Julian McDougall (2005), *The Media Teacher's Book*, Hodder Arnold
Roy Stafford (2001), *Representation,* BFI/*in the picture*

**An additional reading and reference and resources list is available
online at www.bfi.org.uk/tfms.**

Useful websites

www.bbc.co.uk – valuable for information and as an insight into marketing
    and promotion

www.channel4.com

www.barb.co.uk

www.kudosproductions.co.uk

www.companypictures.co.uk (now part of All3Media)

www.itpmag.demon.co.uk – resources on a range of media issues, including
    the magazine *in the picture*

www.screenonline.org.uk – excellent short entries on a range of single TV
    dramas and subgenres. Extracts available for many dramas, especially
    earlier examples

www.imdb.com – useful for production and commercial information as well
    as casting, writers, etc.

www.bfi.org/sightandsound – includes some articles on television and
    broadcasting

www.wikipedia.com – range of articles about TV dramas, broadcasters and
producers

www.aber.ac.uk – resources on a range of media issues

Acknowledgements

Thanks to Glen Creeber for discussing ideas for this book at an early stage and to Stephen Griffiths for sending materials from his University of Staffordshire Televison Drama course.

Thanks to Vivienne Clark and Wendy Earle for their patience and to Nicky North for passing on helpful articles.

And mostly, thanks to Jac for being Jac.